Janice VanCleave's
Science Around the World

Activities on Biomes
from Pole to Pole

WILEY

John Wiley & Sons, Inc.

This book is printed on acid-free paper. ∞

Published by John Wiley & Sons, Inc., Hoboken, New Jersey
Published simultaneously in Canada

Design and production by Navta Associates, Inc.

The publisher and the author have made every reasonable effort to ensure that the experiments and activities in this book are safe when conducted as instructed but assume no responsibility for any damage caused or sustained while performing the experiments or activities in this book. Parents, guardians, and/or teachers should supervise young readers who undertake the experiments and activities in this book.

For general information about our other products and services, please contact our Customer Care Department within the United States at (800) 762-2974, outside the United States at (317) 572-3993 or fax (317) 572-4002.

Wiley also publishes its books in a variety of electronic formats. Some content that appears in print may not be available in electronic books. For more information about Wiley products, visit our web site at www.wiley.com.

ISBN 0-471-20547-8

Printed in the United States of America

V10004051_082718

Contents

Contents

Dedication

This book is dedicated to a very knowledgeable and talented teacher, whose help in writing this book was invaluable. What a pleasure it has been to work with my friend and colleague, Holly Harris.

Acknowledgments

I wish to express my appreciation to these science specialists for their valuable assistance by providing information or assisting me in finding it.

Members of the Central Texas Astronomical Society, including Johnny Barton, John W. McAnally, and Paul Derrick. Johnny is an officer of the club and has been an active amateur astronomer for more than 20 years. John is also on the staff of The Association of Lunar and Planetary Observers where he is acting Assistant Coordinator for Transit Timings of the Jupiter Section. Paul is the author of the "Stargazer" column in the *Waco Tribune-Herald*.

Dr. Glenn S. Orton, a Senior Research Scientist at the Jet Propulsion Laboratory of California Institute of Technology. Glenn is an astronomer and space scientist who specializes in investigating the structure and composition of planetary atmospheres. He is best known for his research on Jupiter and Saturn. I have enjoyed exchanging ideas with Glenn about experiments for modeling astronomy experiments.

Dr. Laura Barge, Senior Research Fellow, CASPER (Center for Astrophysics, Space Physics & Engineering Research). Dr. Ben Doughty, head of the department of physics at Texas A & M University—Commerce in Commerce, Texas. Laura and Ben have helped me to better understand the fun of learning about physics.

Robert Fanick, a chemist at Southwest Research Institute in San Antonio, Texas, and Virginia Malone, a science assessment consultant. These two very special people have provided a great deal of valuable information, which has made this book even more understandable and fun.

Marsha Willis, Middle School Science Coordinator at Region 12 Educational Center, Waco, Texas. Marsha has not only assisted with reviewing activities for this but was instrumental in our being involved in NASA's Texas Fly High Program, which provided us the opportunity for me to fly in NASA's Vomit Comet.

A special note of gratitude to these educators who assisted by pretesting the activities and/or by providing scientific information:

I wish to express my appreciation to James H. Hunderfund, Ed.D.,

Superintendent of Schools, Pamela J. Travis-Moore, Principal, Ron Sineo, Coordinator of Science and Computer Technology, K-8, and William D. Gulick, Science Lead Teacher in Commack Public Schools in Commack, New York. Because of the approval and support of these supervisiors, the following students at Commack Middle School, under the direction of Diane M. Flynn and Ellen M. Vlachos, tested activities in this book: Nicky Alagna, Kelsey Alvarez, Jessica Armentano, Nicholas Baltera, Joseph Biscardi, Taylor Braun, Justin Capozzi, Lauren Celentano, Joseph Costa, Dana D'Aconti, Betsy Daniel, Danielle Marie D'Arcy, Zachary Dean, Andrew Ezzat, Dillon Feigenbaum, Clyvens Fernandez, Michelle Fiorvanti, David Golub, Morgan Golub, Brad Greenstein, Jason Gross, Brooke Gruman, Max Hattenback, Benjamin Hennessy, Craig Isser, Courtney Kitt, Ryan Kopping, Jenna Lanzaro, Danielle Lehmann, Eric Levine, Mike T. Levine, David Lew, Amy Lewis, Matt LoDolce, Joey Lynn, Judy Mandel, Daniel Margolin, Noreen Masciello, Joseph Mileo, Matthew Palazzolo, Shalini Pammal, Leah Peker, Drew Perotti, Joe Pignataro, Jenny Powell, Nicole Ranaldo, Matthew Recio, Alyssa Ridley, Aimee Rizzo, Stefanie Rosenberg, Rob Schumann, Josh Schwartzman, Joshua Seyda, Ashley Naomi St. Preux, Zack Steinbach, Matthew Steinberg, Samantha R. Stern, Michelle Vizzi, Samantha Vulpis, Charlsie Walfish, Kaitlin Watrud, Alison Wohl, Shirou Wu, Michael Young.

I

FORESTS

TROPICAL RAIN FORESTS

DECIDUOUS FORESTS

CONIFEROUS FORESTS

A forest is a terrestrial biome in which trees are the main plant. Although there are exceptions, trees generally are larger than other plants. **Trees** are plants with a **trunk,** which is the main supportive **stem** (part of a plant that supports leaves and flowers) of plants. Trees have woody roots, trunks, and limbs that provide a supportive structure, somewhat like a skeleton, that allows them to grow quite large. The climate, the type of soil, and the **topography** (description of the size, the shape, and the elevation of a region of land) of the region determine the type of trees that make up a forest.

Over 30 percent of Earth's **terrestrial** (land) surface is covered by forests. The three basic types of forests presented in this section are tropical rain forests, deciduous forests, and coniferous forests.

TROPICAL RAIN FORESTS

Rain forests are forests that have a constant warm temperature and receive more than 80 inches (200 cm) of **precipitation** (water that falls from the atmosphere in the form of rain, hail, snow, or sleet) each year in the form of rain. While rain forests are found on different parts of Earth, including the low **elevations** (height above sea level) of mountains, most are found in two regions called the **tropics,** which form a band around the center of Earth. The **northern tropics** region lies between the **equator** (an imaginary line around the center of Earth) and the Tropic of Cancer in the **Northern Hemisphere** (region of Earth that is north of the equator). The **Tropic of Cancer** is located at Latitude 23°N. **Latitude** is an imaginary line

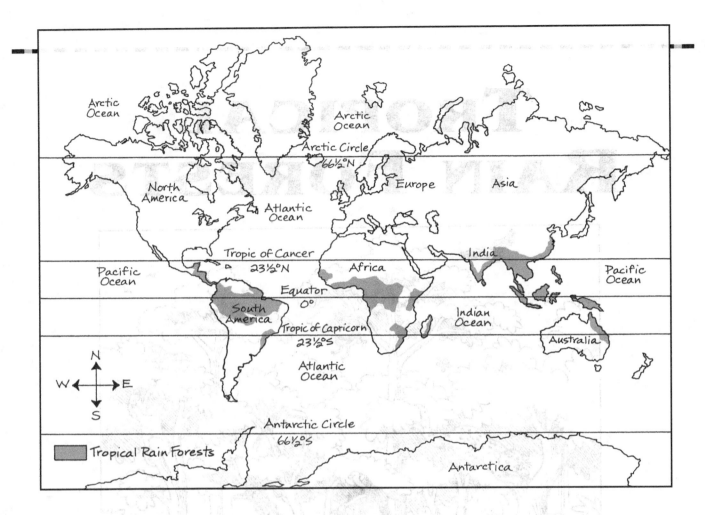

that gives the location of a place north (N) or south (S) of the earth's equator and is expressed in degrees. The **southern tropics** region lies between the equator and the **Tropic of Capricorn** (at 23½°S) in the **Southern Hemisphere** (region of Earth south of the equator).

The rain forests inside and bordering this band that receive more than 80 inches (200 cm) of rain each year are called **tropical rain forests,** and these are the rain forests that will be explored in this book.

The trees and plants of a tropical rain forest are **evergreens** (plants that do not lose all their leaves during the year). Evergreens do lose a few leaves at a time, but new ones are growing as old leaves are shed. In comparison, **deciduous** trees and plants lose all their leaves during part of the year. Huge numbers

of animals live in rain forests, including insects, worms, fish, snakes, lizards, birds, and mammals, such as jaguars, monkeys, and bats. The different rain forests of the world support different kinds of animals.

In this section, you'll identify the locations of rain forests and you'll find out how Earth's rotation affects the temperatures of the tropical areas. **Rotation** is the turning of an object about an **axis** (imaginary line through the center of an object about which the object turns). You'll also discover what soil is and why the soil of such a lush area is lacking in **nutrients** (nourishing materials needed for life). You'll also investigate the **seasons** (divisions of the year defined by the position of Earth as it moves about the Sun, weather, and rainfall), climate, and **organisms** (living things) in rain forests.

Rain Forest Humidity

All forests in the tropics are **tropical forests,** but they are not all rain forests. But, most rain forests are in the tropics. For a forest to be a rain forest, it must receive more than 80 inches (200 cm) of rain each year. Most tropical rain forests receive about 200 inches (500 cm) of rain every year, and a few get more than 400 inches (1,000 cm).

While the rainfall in most tropical rain forests is evenly spaced throughout the year, the tropical areas of India, Myanmar (formerly known as Burma), and Southeast Asia along the northern Indian Ocean coasts experience a cycle of seasonal changes related to rain called **wet seasons** and **dry seasons.** Wet seasons are times of abundant rain, and dry seasons are times when there is a lack of rain. Tropical rain forests in these areas are called **monsoon rain forests** (areas that experience pronounced wet and dry seasons). Unlike most tropical rain forests, which are evergreen forests, many plants in monsoon rain forests are deciduous, which means they lose all their leaves during part of the year. The leaves are lost during the dry season.

The consistently high temperatures and abundant rainfall in rain forests result in another characteristic of this type of forest— high humidity. **Humidity** is the measure of the amount of water **vapor** (gaseous state of a substance, such as water, that is normally in a liquid state) in the air. The air in a rain forest is like a sponge; it holds lots of water vapor. While rainfall is a major contributor to humidity, transpiration also affects humidity. **Transpiration** is the **evaporation** (change from a liquid to a gas) of water from a plant's **stomata** (tiny surface openings that are especially abundant on the undersides of **leaves,** the main food-producing part of a plant).

FUN TIME!

Purpose

To measure relative humidity.

Materials

cotton ball
tap water
2 outdoor thermometers that measure in
   Celsius degrees
transparent tape
index card (handheld battery-operated fan
   can be used)

Procedure

1. Wet the cotton ball with water and wrap it around the bulb of one of the thermometers. This is your wet-bulb thermometer. Leave the second thermometer uncovered. This is your dry-bulb thermometer.

2. Lay the two thermometers on a table with their bulbs extended over the table edge. Tape the other ends of the thermometers to the table.

3. Use the index card to fan the air near the bulbs of the two thermometers. Do not hit the bulbs with the card. *Note: If a battery-operated fan is used, hold it so that the blades*

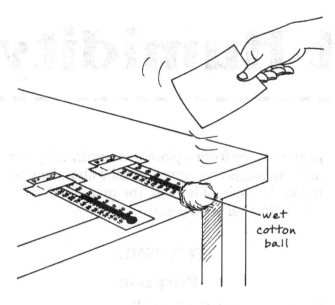

of the fan are about 4 inches (10 cm) from the thermometer bulbs.

4. Continue to fan the bulbs until the temperature on the wet-bulb thermometer stops decreasing. Then record the Celsius temperatures from both thermometers.

5. Use the following example and the relative humidity table to determine the relative humidity from your temperature readings.

Example:

What is the relative humidity if the dry-bulb reading is 16°C and the wet-bulb reading is 13°C?

- Subtract the wet-bulb temperature from the dry-bulb temperature:

$$16°C - 13°C = 3°C$$

- Find the dry-bulb temperature (16°), in the column on the left side of the Relative Humidity in Air table. Now find the difference between the two thermometer readings (3°) in the horizontal row at the top

of the table. Where the column and the row meet is the number for the relative humidity. For this example, the number is 71; thus the relative humidity is 71 percent.

Relative Humidity in Air

Difference between Dry-Bulb and Wet-Bulb Temperatures (C°)

Dry-Bulb Temperature (C°)	1	2	3	4	5	6	7	8	9	10	11	12	13	14	15	16
0	81	64	46	29	13											
2	84	68	52	37	22	7										
4	85	71	57	43	29	16										
6	86	73	60	48	35	24	11									
8	87	75	63	51	40	29	19	8								
10	88	77	66	55	44	34	24	15	6							
12	89	78	68	58	48	39	29	21	12							
14	90	79	70	60	51	42	34	26	18	10						
16	90	81	71	63	54	46	38	30	23	15	8					
18	91	82	73	65	57	49	41	34	27	20	14	7				
20	91	83	74	66	59	51	44	37	31	24	18	12	6			
22	92	83	76	68	61	54	47	40	34	28	22	17	11	6		
24	92	84	77	69	62	56	49	43	37	31	26	20	15	10	5	
26	92	85	78	71	64	58	51	46	40	34	29	24	19	14	10	5

Results

You made a wet-bulb and dry-bulb thermometer and used them to measure relative humidity.

Why?

Relative humidity is the amount of water vapor in the air compared to the total amount of vapor that the air could hold at that temperature, expressed as a percentage. An instrument, like the one you made in this experiment, which contains a wet-bulb and a dry-bulb thermometer and is used to measure relative humidity, is called a **psychrometer.**

When the relative humidity reaches 100 percent, the air is **saturated,** meaning it cannot hold any more water vapor. If air with 100 percent humidity cools, some of the water vapor in the air will **condense** (change from a gas to a liquid). If the air is next to the ground, the extra moisture will condense as dew. **Dew** is water from water vapor in the air that condenses on cool surfaces. Above the ground, the extra moisture will condense into **cloud droplets** (tiny drops of water with diameters between 0.00004 to 0.002 inches [0.0001 and 0.005 cm] that form clouds). **Clouds** are visible masses of water droplets that float in the air, usually high above the earth. **Fog** is a cloud that is close to the ground. Raindrops can form in clouds by **accretion,** which is the merging of water drops that bump into one another. When the drops get large enough they fall. Raindrops also form if tiny ice **crystals** (solid materials whose particles are arranged in a repeating pattern) and water drops are mixed together in a cloud. The water sticks to the ice and the ice crystals grow large and become heavy enough to fall. As they fall they melt and hit the ground as rain.

MORE FUN WITH HUMIDITY!

Animals, as well as plants, add water to the air. See how the breath of animals increases air humidity. Do this by placing the end of a drinking straw inside the opening of a quart-size resealable plastic bag. Seal the bag as much as possible around the straw. Exhale through the straw five or more times, then quickly pull the straw out of the bag and completely seal the bag. Observe how cloudy the inside of the bag becomes. If the bag is not cloudy, repeat the procedure of blowing through the straw then removing the straw and closing the bag. Rub the outside of the bag with your fingers. The

cloudiness will disappear and tiny drops of water will form. Rubbing the bag causes the tiny invisible drops of water clouding the bag to combine into larger visible drops. If the drops of water are not visible, open the bag and feel the inside with your fingers.

BOOK LIST

Allaby, Michael. *How the Weather Works.* Pleasantville, New York: Reader's Digest, 1995. Information and experiments that let you discover more about the weather, including humidity.

Christian, Spencer. *Can It Really Rain Frogs?* New York: Wiley, 1997. Information and experiments about humidity and other weather events.

VanCleave, Janice. *Weather.* New York: Wiley, 1995. Experiments about humidity and other weather-related topics. Each chapter contains ideas that can be turned into award-winning science fair projects.

Rain Forest Soil

Soil is the top layer of Earth's surface that supports plant life. It is composed of particles from rock mixed with **humus** (material in soil formed by decayed plants and animals). **Fertile soil** contains an abundance of humus, thus it contains an abundance of nutrients needed for plant growth.

Decomposition is the breakdown of substances into simpler parts, such as the decay of plants and animals. The rate of decomposition of dead plants and animals in a tropical rain forest is very fast. For example, if it took 12 months for a plant to decay in an area of Texas where much of the year is hot and dry, it might take only 6 weeks for the same plant to decay in an area of a tropical rain forest where it is hot and wet year-round. Even though there is rapid decomposition and an abundance of materials being decomposed, very few of the nutrients accumulate in the soil of tropical rain forests. Instead, they are quickly absorbed by plants or washed away by rain.

Because the soil of tropical rain forests is so nutrient-poor, areas cleared for growing **crops** (plants grown for food) are soon not very productive. As the nutrients in the soil are used up, planters move on to cut down more rain forest trees. Because of this, as more of the tropical rain forest is destroyed, more barren infertile land is produced.

FUN TIME!

Purpose

To demonstrate the loss of nutrients in tropical rain forest soil.

Materials

marking pen

9-ounce (270-mL) paper cup

six 5-ounce (150-mL) paper cups

pencil

round coffee filter

1 cup (250-mL) soil from outdoors (potting soil will work)

red food coloring

3-ounce (90-mL) paper cup

tap water

Procedure

1. Using the marking pen, label the large cup "soil" and the six 5-ounce (150-mL) cups with numbers 1 through 6.

2. Use the pencil point to make 15 or more small holes in the bottom of the soil cup. Line the inside bottom of the lower half of this cup with the coffee filter.

3. Place the soil inside the filter-lined soil cup.

4. Add 5 drops of food coloring to the soil in the cup.

5. Stand the soil cup in cup number 1.

6. Fill the 3-ounce (90-mL) cup with water, then pour the water into the soil cup.

7. Allow the water to drain out of the soil-filled cup and into cup number 1.

8. Repeat steps 5 through 7 five times, using the remaining five cups.

soil

coffee filter

holes in bottom of cup

Soil

5

6

4

3

1

9. Compare the color of the water in each cup. How does the color of the drained water in cup 1 compare to that in cup 6?

Results

The water in cup 1 is very red, but the redness of the water in each of the later cups decreases, so that by cup 6 it is very pale or not present at all.

Why?

The red food coloring represents nutrients in the soil of a tropical rain forest. The water draining out of the cup containing the soil represents surface **runoff** (rainwater that is unable to soak into the ground and moves over its surface). Nutrients in the soil that are **soluble** (able to **dissolve**—break up and thoroughly mix with another substance) mix with this water and are transported to nearby water-

ways, such as streams or rivers. The decrease in the color of the draining water indicates that as more and more rain flows across the soil, the soil's nutrients can be washed away. This process of washing away nutrients is called **leaching.**

MORE FUN WITH SOIL!

You can grow some plants for a time in **infertile soil** (soil lacking nutrients). If you plant a carrot top in sand, for example, food stored in the plant will be used to form leaves. Once the leaves are formed, they will produce food by **photosynthesis** (process by which plants use chlorophyll and light energy, generally sunlight, to manufacture food from water and **carbon dioxide**, a gas in the air).

Start by filling a small flowerpot or large paper cup about three-fourths full with clean sand, such as from an aquarium. Select a carrot with stems (part of a plant that support the leaves and flowers and transports nutrients) and leaves. The shorter the stems the better. Ask an adult to cut off ½ inch (1.25 cm) of the carrot's top. Place the cut end of the carrot's top on the surface of the sand. Push the top about ¼ inch (0.63 cm) below the surface of the sand. Use a spray bottle to spray the surface of the sand to moisten it, but do not make it dripping wet. Check the surface of the soil periodically and add water as necessary to keep it moist. Place the cup near a window with direct sunlight. Watch the top of the vegetable grow.

Determine how long your plant will grow in the infertile sand. You may wish to try growing different vegetable tops, such as celery or red beets.

BOOK LIST

Dietl, Ulla. *The Plant-and-Grow Project Book*. New York: Sterling Publishing, 1995. Ideas for using soil and other mediums for growing different kinds of plants.

VanCleave, Janice. *Ecology for Every Kid*. New York: Wiley, 1996. Fun, simple ecology experiments, including information about soil and soil management.

Rain Forest Plants

Although tropical rain forests cover only about 7 percent of Earth's surface, they provide a home for more **species** (specific types of organisms) of plants and animals than all other biomes combined. A 2.5-acre (1-hectare) patch of Brazilian rain forest contains more than 400 tree species; in the same-size area of a forest in mid-North America, there are only 2 to 20 tree species.

Because there are generally no unfavorable growing periods in the rain forest, the trees are evergreen, meaning they have leaves all year long. Most rain forest trees are **broadleaf,** meaning their leaves are broad and flat. Trees are a **woody plant** (a plant with a large amount of wood). **Wood** is the part of a plant made of **xylem tubes** (tubes that transport water and other nutrients from the root throughout a plant and provide support); it is the hard, tough substance that forms the trunks and **branches** (stems that grow out of a trunk) of trees. Woods from broadleaf trees are called **hardwoods.** While wood from most hardwood trees is physically hard, some, such as Balsa wood, is not. The classification of hardwood indicates what kind of xylem tubes it has. Hardwood trees have two types of xylem. One is made of long, narrow tubes. The other is made of large vessels with extra fibers running through them for support. These fibers tend to make the wood hard, thus wood from broadleafed trees is called hardwood. The xylem of **softwood** trees, including **conifers** (plants with seed-bearing structures called **cones**) such as pines and firs, does not have the larger vessels, thus these trees generally have physically soft wood.

The types of plants in a tropical rain forest are arranged in layers, or levels. These layers vary somewhat from one area to another, and the boundaries of each layer are not distinct. But in all tropical rain forests, there are four basic layers. In order, from top to the bottom, these layers are called emergent, canopy, sub-canopy, and forest floor.

The plants in the **emergent layer** (a rain forest's upper layer, made up of the tallest trees) are trees generally about 115 to 150 feet (34.5 to 45 m) tall. These trees rise about 30 feet (9 m) or more above the other trees in the forest. Broadleaf trees, such as teak and mahogany, are found here. There are usually only one or two of these giant trees per acre of forest. The emergent trees usually have small leaves, umbrella-shaped crowns, and tall, thin trunks that are supported by strong props, such as stilted roots and buttresses. **Roots** are the part of a plant that anchors it in the ground. **Stilted roots** start at about 3 to 4 feet (0.9 to 1.2 m) high on the trunk and grow down into the ground. **Buttresses** are thick roots that spread horizontally just above the ground. Because trees in the emergent layer stick up above the other trees, they often endure changing temperatures, low humidity, and strong winds.

FUN TIME!
Purpose

To make a model of a tree buttress.

Materials

pencil

plastic ruler

two 4-by-12-inch (10-by-30-cm) pieces of cardboard, such as the back of a writing tablet

scissors

grape-sized piece of clay

transparent tape

Procedure

1. Use the pencil and the ruler to draw a vertical line down the center of one of the pieces of cardboard. Draw a buttress shape, as shown, on the cardboard with the highest part of the buttress crossing the vertical line.

2. Use the ruler and pencil to make a dot halfway between the highest point on the buttress and its bottom edge, which is the bottom edge of the cardboard, as shown.

3. Cut out the buttress shape.

4. Lay the cardboard buttress on the other piece of cardboard. Trace the buttress onto the cardboard, then cut out the second buttress shape.

5. On one buttress, make a cut from the highest point of the top edge to the dot halfway down. On the second buttress, cut from the bottom edge below the dot all the way up to the dot.

6. Fit the two buttresses together at a 90-degree angle to form a three-dimensional model.

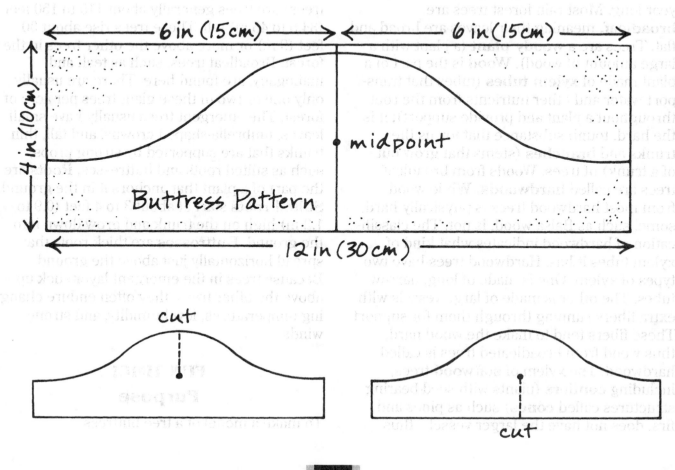

7. Make a ball out of the clay. Put the ball on a table and push the ruler into the clay so the ruler stands upright. Face the wide side of the ruler and blow toward the top to determine if it is easy to push the ruler over.

8. Stand the ruler back up with the clay, but this time place the buttress model next to the ruler. Tape the ruler to the model.

9. Again blow on the ruler to determine if it is easy to push the ruler over.

Results

The ruler is more easily blown over when not secured to the buttress model.

Why?

The trees in tropical rain forests have shallow roots. Some of the emergent trees have buttresses. Buttresses provide extra support at the base of the tall emergent trees. Without this support, they, like the ruler, would be more easily pushed over by the wind.

MORE FUN WITH TREES!

Some emergent trees in the rain forest grow to be 200 feet (60 m) tall. How does the height of the trees where you live compare to these rain forest giants? On a sunny day, pick out a tree that has a clear shadow on the ground. Measure the length of the tree's shadow from the base of the tree to the end of the shadow in inches (cm). Call this length L_1. Then stand so that you cast a clear shadow on the ground and ask a helper to measure the length of your shadow in inches (cm). Call this length L_2. Measure your height in inches (cm) and call it H_2. Use the following equation to determine the height of the tree, which is called H_1.

$$H_1 = (H_2 \times L_1) \div L_2$$

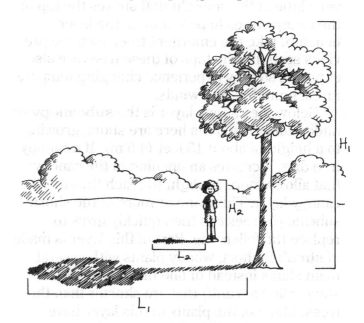

BOOK LIST

Braithwaite, Althea. *Trees and Leaves.* New York: Troll, 1990. Information about different kinds of trees and their leaves. Includes information about organisms found in trees.

Milford, Susan. *The Kids Nature Book.* Charlotte, Vermont: Williamson Publishing, 1996. Indoor and outdoor activities and experiments, including those about trees.

VanCleave, Janice. *Ecology for Every Kid.* New York: Wiley, 1996. Fun, simple ecology experiments, including information about forest biomes.

Forest Canopy and Below

A rain forest's second layer is called the **canopy layer** or roof. This layer is formed by flat-crowned trees generally between 65 and 100 feet (19.5 and 30 m) tall. The network of branches and leaves from these trees forms an umbrellalike covering over the forest, allowing very little of the sunlight that strikes the top of the canopy trees to penetrate to the layer beneath. Like the emergent trees (see the previous section), the tops of these trees are also exposed, so they experience changing temperatures, humidity, and winds.

Below the canopy layer is the **subcanopy** or understory. The trees here are short, growing to a height of about 15 feet (4.5 m). If a canopy tree dies, it creates an opening in the canopy that allows more sunlight to reach the subcanopy layer. Then, one or more of the shorter subcanopy trees can then quickly grow to replace the fallen one. Part of this layer is made of **shrubs** (short, woody plants with several main stems instead of one main supportive stem called a trunk) that are shorter than the trees. Many of the plants in this layer have large leaves that help them catch almost every ray of sunlight that reaches them.

The **forest floor** layer, the bottom layer, in contrast to the canopy layer, is still and dark. The temperature and humidity there is always high and relatively constant. People sometimes assume that a tropical rain forest is filled with the remains of fallen trees, branches, and leaves. But the truth is that the floor of a tropi-

cal rain forest is basically open and uncluttered. This is because so little sunlight reaches the floor that only a few small plants can survive, and when any plant dies it quickly decomposes on the dark, damp forest floor. Only along open areas, such as where the forests have been cut or along a riverbank, is the undergrowth so thick that it is like a jungle.

FUN TIME!
Purpose

To determine how tree leaf size affects sunlight on a forest's floor.

Materials

sheet of green construction paper
pencil
scissors
tape
2 green pipe cleaners (found at craft stores)
desk lamp

Procedure

1. Fold the paper in half by placing the short ends together, then unfold it. Cut along the fold.

2. On one of the pieces of paper, draw a picture of a leaf as big as possible with a point at one end, as shown. Cut out the leaf.

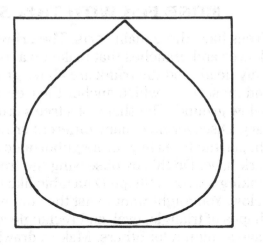

3. Fold the other piece of paper in half two times, first from top to bottom then from side to side.

4. Draw two leaves on the folded paper. Cut out the leaves, cutting through all four layers.

5. Make a model of a canopy tree stem with one leaf by taping the large leaf to the end of one of the pipe cleaners.

6. Make a model of a stem from an emergent tree by taping one small leaf to one end of the remaining pipe cleaner. Tape the other small leaves along the sides of the pipe cleaner, as shown.

7. Hold the stem models side by side under the light of the desk lamp. Observe how much light hits the desk under each model.

Results

There is a large shadow beneath the stem with one large leaf, and small shadows with light showing among them beneath the stem with eight small leaves.

Why?

The trees in the emergent layer grow separately from one another so their leaves do not overlap and block sunlight from plants below. They also have small leaves on their stems, allowing sunlight to pass through as in the emergent tree model in this experiment. But the trees of the canopy layer are very close together, and many have large leaves, like the one in this activity. Each leaf not only blocks a great deal of light, but is crowded together with other leaves so they form an umbrella that blocks most of the light from reaching the next layer down. The pointed tip aids in the flow of rainwater off the leaves.

MORE FUN WITH TREES!

Trees have three main parts. The **crown** (leaves and branches that make up a tree's leafy head) and the trunk are above ground, and most roots, which anchor the tree, are below ground. The shape of a tree's crown can vary. Discover how many different crown shapes the trees in your neighborhood or local park have. Do this by observing the trees and making a Crown Shape Data table like the one below. You might want to list the common shapes of triangle, oval, and rectangle and then have a column for others. Make a drawing of each shape you observe.

BOOK LIST

Bernard, Robin. *Rain Forest.* New York: Scholastic, 1995. Information and hands-on activities about rain forests, including the layering of the forest plants.

National Wildlife Federation. *Rain Forests: Tropical Treasures.* New York: Learning Triangle Press, 1997. Activities, games, and information about tropical rain forests.

Taylor, Barbara. *Rain Forest.* New York: DK Publishing, 1998. Photographs and information about the living organisms of rain forests.

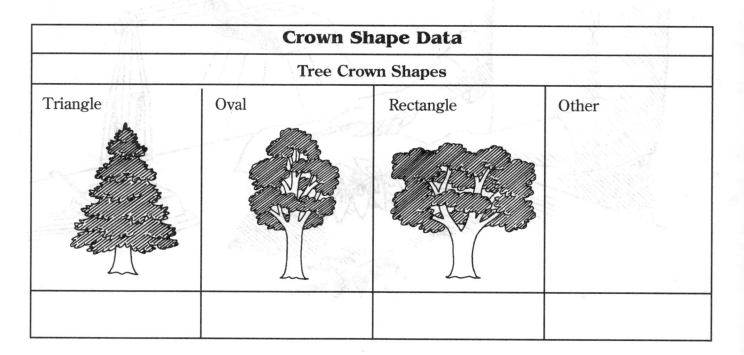

Crown Shape Data			
Tree Crown Shapes			
Triangle	Oval	Rectangle	Other

5

Rain Forest Animals

More than half of the different species of animals on Earth make their home in tropical rain forests, including as many as 30 million insect species. The types of animals found in a rain forest vary from layer to layer. Starting at the top emergent layer, the animals you might find include harpy eagles, howler monkeys, flying insects, insect-eating snakes, and bats.

The canopy layer houses the majority of the animals found in a tropical rain forest. This is because it contains an abundance of food, such as fruits and leaves. It also provides shelter for animals, such as spider monkeys, sloths, tree frogs, the margay cat, ants, beetles, bats, toucans, parrots, hummingbirds, the tailorbird, snakes, and lizards. Many of these animals never touch the forest floor during their entire lifetime.

The shaded area of the subcanopy (a forest's layer beneath the canopy) is the home of many flowering plants that provide food or homes for such animals as butterflies, termites, toads, frogs, snakes, lizards, beetles, and parakeets. The rain forest floor receives such a small amount of sunlight that few flowering plants can grow here. But there are edible roots and tubers (underground food-storing stems) as well as dead plant matter. Animals found here include armadillos, peccaries, slugs, termites, beetles, centipedes, and cockroaches.

The same animals are not found in all rain forests. Some are specific to a certain geographic location, such as lemurs in Madagascar, poison arrow frogs in South America, and the pitohui in New Guinea. (The pitohui's flesh and feathers contain a deadly poison.) Different apes are found in different areas, such as gibbons in southeast Asia, orangutans in Sumatra and Borneo, and gorillas, the largest, and most powerful ape, in Africa.

Tropical rain forests house giant versions of many animals, such as the Costa Rican cockroach, which can grow larger than your hand; the African swallowtail butterfly, with a 10-inch (25-cm) wingspan; and the python of southeast Asia, one of the largest snakes, which reaches lengths of up to 33 feet (11 m).

FUN TIME!

Purpose

To model the nest building of a tailorbird.

Materials

scissors
12-inch (30-cm) piece of string
large green leaf
pointed tweezers

Procedure

1. Cut the string into pieces about 2 inches (10 cm) long.

2. Fold the leaf in half by placing the sides together.

3. Use the pointed ends of the tweezers to punch a hole near the edge and through both layers of the leaf.

4. Using the tweezer ends, which have been poked through the two layers of the folded leaf, pinch the end of one of the strings and pull half of the string through the holes.

5. Make another hole with the tweezers through the two layers of the folded leaf near the first one and pull one of the ends of the string through the second hole.

6. Repeat steps 3 through 5, using a second string.

7. Continue making holes with the tweezers and pulling strings through the holes until the edges of the leaf are sewn together.

Results

The edges of the leaf are sewn together.

Why?

The tiny tailorbird bird lives in the canopy layer of tropical rain forests in Southeast Asia. This bird got its name because it sews together the

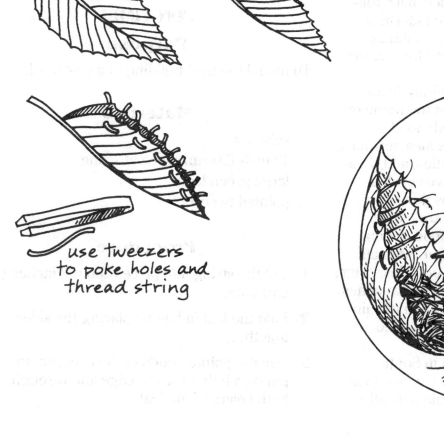

fold up sides of leaf

use tweezers to poke holes and thread string

edges of leaves to hold its cocoonlike nest. In this investigation, you used tweezers and string to sew a leaf together. The strings are not tied together but instead are pulled through two sets of holes in an effort to hold the leaf together. The tailorbird uses its beak and plant fibers, silk from spiderwebs, or any available threadlike material to make its nest. The tailorbird uses its beak to bend one large leaf or several smaller leaves in half and to punch holes through the edges of the leaf. It then draws the fibers through the holes to sew the edges of the leaf together. The bird then puts more fibers inside the leaf to make a nest in which the female lays three eggs.

MORE FUN WITH BIRDS!

The canopy of tropical rain forests is the leafiest layer, so it attracts the most insects and the most insect-eating birds. You can attract seed-eating birds and observe their behavior by providing them with food. Build a bird feeder using a thin plastic bottle with a lid, such as a soda bottle. Ask an adult to cut two 2-by-2-inch (5-by-5-cm) windows on either side at about 3 inches (7.5 cm) above the bottom of the bottle. Ask an adult to cut holes below each window. You need holes large enough to push a stick, small wooden dowel, or pencil through to form a perch for the birds. Once the stick is in place, fill the bottle up to the window opening with birdseed.

Put the lid on the bottle and tie a string around its neck. Hang the bird feeder outside near a window where you can observe it. Keep fresh birdseed in the container.

BOOK LIST

Dennis, John V. and Michael McKinley. *How to Attract Birds*. San Ramon, Cal.: The Solaris Group, 1995. Information on how to attract birds by offering the materials they need for survival.

National Wildlife Federation. *Birds, Birds, Birds*. New York: Learning Triangle Press, 1997. Activities, games, and information about birds, including those in tropical rain forests.

DECIDUOUS FORESTS

A **deciduous forest** is a biome characterized by deciduous trees, which are trees that lose all their leaves during part of the year. Though most of the trees in this kind of forest are deciduous, there are also some evergreen trees, such as pine, which retain individual leaves for one or more consecutive years. The farther north the forest is, the greater the number of evergreens will be. This type of forest has five layers. The upper layer is made up of the tallest trees, such as oak, beech, and maple. Holly, willows, hazel, and other shorter trees make up the second layer, and shrubs form the middle, or third, layer. The fourth layer is the herb layer of short plants, including flowers and ferns, and the ground layer contains ground cover, including plants like mosses. This forest is a home to large animals such as bears, deer, and wolves. Some of the small animals that live here include snakes, squirrels, rabbits, rac-

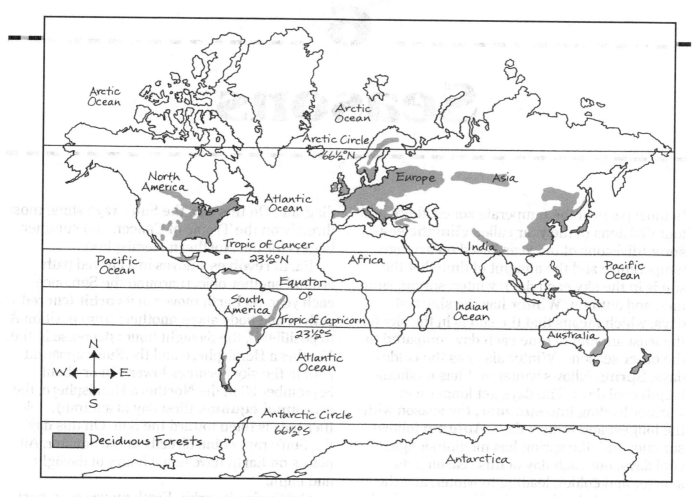

coons, and opossums. Many birds live in deciduous forests during the warmer parts of the year but move south during colder months.

Deciduous forests are found at low to medium elevations on mountains and in the **temperate zones** (regions north and south of the tropics). Deciduous forests in the temperate zones are also called **temperate deciduous forests.** This region has a **temperate climate,** which is a climate without extremes in temperature or precipitation and with cool winters and warm summers of about equal length. North of the equator is the **north temperate zone,** which is the region between the Tropic of Cancer (at 23½°N latitude) and the **Arctic Circle** (at 66½°N latitude). South of the equator is the **south temperate zone,** which is the region between the Tropic of Capricorn (at 23½°S latitude) and the **Antarctic Circle**

(at 66½°S latitude). In these areas, temperatures average between –13°F and 100°F (–25°C and 38°C) and the average yearly rainfall is 30 to 60 inches (75 to 150 cm).

Unlike the tropics, the temperate zones have changing seasons as a result of changes in temperature. Most deciduous forests are found in the two temperate zones, with the majority of them being in the northern temperate zone located in eastern North America, Europe, and Asia. There are some deciduous regions in the Southern Hemisphere, but their plants and animals are different from those in the northern deciduous forests.

In this section, you'll look at the northern temperate deciduous forests, the seasons in the forests, and the broadleaf trees. You'll also learn why leaves change color and how they transpire, and discuss some of the organisms that live in these deciduous forests.

6

Seasons

In most parts of the temperate zones, there are four divisions of the year called **climatic seasons** (divisions of the year based on average temperature and the amount of time that the sun is in the sky each day): winter, spring, summer, and autumn. **Winter** has the shortest days, which means that the sun is in the sky for the least amount of time each day compared to the other seasons. Winter also has the coldest days. **Spring** follows winter and has medium-length cool days. The days get longer and warmer leading into **summer,** the season with the longest and hottest days. **Autumn** follows summer and like spring has medium-length cool days, but each day of this season gets shorter and colder, leading to winter, and the seasonal cycle begins again. The seasons in the temperate zone of the Northern Hemisphere are the opposite of those in the temperate zone of the Southern Hemisphere. This means that when it is spring in the Northern Hemisphere, it is autumn in the Southern Hemisphere.

Seasons based on climate are affected by changes in the amount of sunlight Earth receives and the angle of the sunlight hitting Earth. Direct or perpendicular sunlight warms the atmosphere the most. Sunlight that is more angled warms the atmosphere the least. The angle of sunlight for each region on Earth depends on the position of Earth in relation to the Sun. The Earth's axis is at a tilt of 23½° in relation to its orbit around the Sun. In the Northern Hemisphere, the **summer solstice** (first day of summer) occurs on or about June 21, when the North Pole has its greatest tilt toward the Sun, as shown in position A in the diagram. On this day, the Sun's rays shine most directly on the Tropic of Cancer, and summer begins for the Northern Hemisphere.

Earth **revolves** (moves in a curved path around another object) around the Sun once each year. As Earth moves in its **orbit** (curved path of one body about another) from position A to position B, the daylight hours decrease in the Northern Hemisphere and the Sun's apparent path in the sky becomes lower. On or about September 23 in the Northern Hemisphere, the **autumnal equinox** (first day of autumn), neither pole is tilted toward the Sun. On this day the Sun's rays shine directly at the equator. All places on Earth have equal hours of daylight and night.

Continuing its orbit, Earth moves from position B to C. During this time the North Pole tilts farther away from the Sun each day, and in the Northern Hemisphere the days become shorter. On or about December 22 marks the **winter solstice,** the first day of winter and the shortest day of the year in the Northern Hemisphere, when the North Pole is tilted farthest from the Sun. The Sun's path is lowest in the sky and the Sun's rays shine most directly on the Tropic of Capricorn in the Southern Hemisphere.

Each day as Earth moves from position C to D, the days in the Northern Hemisphere become longer and the Sun's path rises a little higher in the sky. On or about March 21, the **vernal equinox,** as on the autumnal equinox, neither pole is tilted toward the Sun. Again, on this day all places on Earth have 12 hours of daylight. This marks the beginning of spring in the Northern Hemisphere. As Earth continues

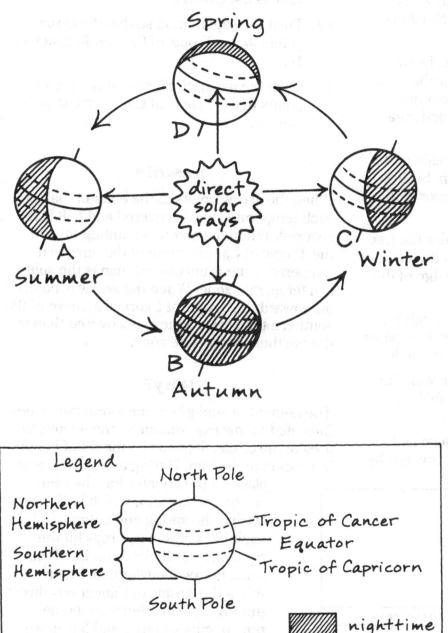

Northern Hemisphere Seasons

Spring

D

direct solar rays

A
Summer

C
Winter

B
Autumn

Legend

North Pole

Northern Hemisphere {
Southern Hemisphere {

Tropic of Cancer
Equator
Tropic of Capricorn

South Pole

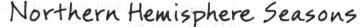 nighttime

FUN TIME!

Purpose

To determine how much sunlight the northern and southern temperate zones have during different seasons.

Materials

drawing compass
8-by-8-inch (20-by-20-cm) square piece of poster board or any stiff paper
scissors
pencil
ruler
3-by-7-inch (7.5-by-17.5-cm) piece of black construction paper
9-by-12-inch (22.5-by-30-cm) sheet of yellow construction paper
transparent tape
paper brad

Procedure

1. Use the compass to draw a circle 6 inches (15 cm) in diameter on the poster board. Cut out the circle.

2. Use the pencil and ruler to draw two perpendicular lines across the cutout circle. Label one of the lines Equator. The other line represents Earth's axis.

3. Draw two lines parallel to the equator line, one line ¾ inch (1.9 cm) above and the other line 2¼ inches (5.6 cm) above the equator. Use the pencil to shade the area between the two lines.

its journey there is more sunlight each day in the Northern Hemisphere. On or about June 21, Earth reaches position A, thus completing its yearly orbit around the Sun, and heads toward position B again.

4. Label the line near the equator Tropic of Cancer and the other Arctic Circle, as shown. Label the shaded area Northern Temperate Zone.

5. Repeat step 3, drawing the lines below the equator line. Label the line near the equator Tropic of Capricorn and the other Antarctic Circle. Label the shaded area Southern Temperate Zone.

6. Lay the black paper on the left side of the yellow sheet of paper, as shown. Secure the short edges of the black paper with tape.

7. Slip half of the paper circle under the free edge of the black paper so that the equator line is perpendicular with the edge of the black paper.

8. Use a pencil to make a hole through the center of the paper circle and yellow paper. Insert the paper brad through the hole.

9. On the yellow paper and in line with the equator, draw a large arrow. Label the arrow Direct Rays.

10. Notice how much of the northern and southern temperate zones are covered by the black paper and how much of each zone is not covered.

11. Turn the paper circle so that the arrow points to the Tropic of Cancer. Repeat step 10.

12. Turn the paper circle so that the arrow points to the Tropic of Capricorn. Repeat step 10.

Results

When the arrow points to the equator, half of each temperate zone is covered and half is not covered. When the arrow is pointing toward the Tropic of Cancer, more of the northern temperate zone is uncovered than is the southern temperate zone. When the arrow is pointing toward the Tropic of Capricorn, more of the southern temperate zone is uncovered than is the northern temperate zone.

Why?

The amount of sunlight in the temperate zones, indicated in this experiment by the uncovered area of the circle, depends on the tilt of Earth in relation to the Sun. During any season, any place on the equator has the same amount of daylight, which is 12 hours. During the spring and autumn equinoxes, direct sun rays hit the equator, and all places on Earth have equal hours of daylight and night. When the Tropic of Cancer has direct sun rays, the northern temperate zone begins summer and has more daylight hours than the southern temperate zone, which begins winter. When the Tropic of Capricorn has direct sun rays, the northern temperate zone begins winter and has fewer daylight hours than the southern temperate zone, which begins summer.

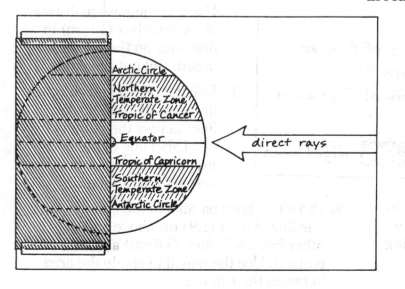

MORE FUN WITH THE EARTH'S TILT!

The tilt of one end of Earth's axis toward or away from the Sun is due to the position of Earth in its orbit around the Sun. The axis itself doesn't change direction. Demonstrate this by placing a chair in an open area of a room. The chair represents the Sun. Hold a broom or long stick in your hand so that it is tilted. The broom represents the axis of Earth. Stand facing the chair and point the upper end of the broom handle toward the wall behind the chair. In order to walk forward during your trip around the chair, you will have to turn your body and reposition your hands on the broom, but don't change the direction in which the broom is pointing or how it is tilted. The straw end of the broom represents the South Pole, and the North Pole is the end of the broom's handle. Note when the North Pole and South Pole tilt away and toward the Sun (chair). The **South Pole** and **North Pole** are the south and north ends, respectively, of Earth's axis.

BOOK LIST

Moché, Dinah. *Astronomy Today.* New York: Random House, 1995. Information about planets, stars, and space exploration, including facts about seasons.

VanCleave, Janice. *Geography for Every Kid.* New York: Wiley, 1993. Fun, simple geography experiments, including information about seasons.

Watt, Fiona. *Planet Earth.* London: Usborne, 1991. Information, projects, and activities about Earth, including ones about seasons.

START

Broadleaf Trees

Most deciduous trees are broadleaf (have leaves that are broad and flat), such as hickory, maple, beech, and some oaks, and a few are conifers, such as the larch. Woods from broadleaf trees are called hardwoods and woods from conifers (plants with seed-bearing structures called cones) are called softwoods, regardless of their actual hardness. (A **seed** is the part of a plant from which a new plant grows.)

While the wood of most broadleaf trees is hard and useful for making sturdy furniture, some broadleaf trees, such as cottonwoods and magnolias, have soft wood. The same is true of coniferous trees. Most have soft wood, but some, such as yellow pines and yews, have very hard wood.

The trunk of a broadleaf tree does not reach the top of the tree. Instead it divides into spreading branches that form the tree's crown. If a tree is by itself and not crowded by other trees, its crown's shape can be identified. For example, oaks have a wide spreading crown, while poplars have a tall, narrow crown.

Broadleaf trees are the largest angiosperms. **Angiosperms** are flowering plants. They have flowers and fruit, which contain their seeds. A few flowering trees, such as magnolia, dogwood, and cherry, have very attractive flowers. But most tree flowers are tiny and dull colored.

Leaves grow from a point on the stem called a **node.** On the stem, broad leaves are positioned in an organized arrangement that results in the stem's being balanced. The common leaf arrangements of trees are opposite and alternate. Leaves are in an **opposite** arrangement pattern when two leaves grow from the same node, one on either side of the stem. Ash, aspen, ailanthus, and red maples have opposite-leaf arrangements. An **alternate** arrangement is one in which one leaf grows from each node in a stair-step pattern from one side to the other along the stem. Oak, elm, birch, and poplar have an alternate-leaf arrangement.

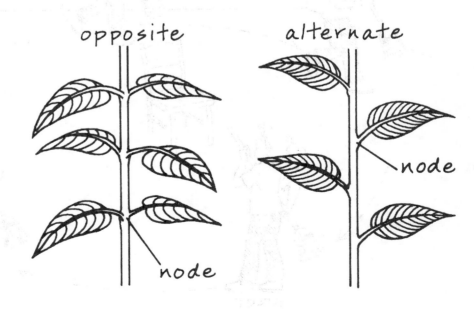

opposite   alternate

node   node

FUN TIME!

Purpose

To determine how the placement of leaves on a branch affects it balance.

Materials

3-by-5-inch (7.5-by-12.5-cm) index card
pencil
scissors
drinking straw
12-inch (30-cm) dowel with a diameter about half that of the straw (a wooden skewer will work)
4 or more books
transparent tape

Procedure

1. Fold the index card in half by placing the short sides together. Draw a leaf as large as possible that is 3 inches (7.5 cm) long on one side.

2. Cut out the leaf, cutting through both layers of the card. You should have two identical leaf shapes.

3. Cut a 4-inch (10-cm) piece from the straw.

4. Make two stacks of books and set them about 8 inches (20 cm) apart.

5. Insert the dowel through the piece of straw and place the ends of the skewer on the edges of the books, as shown. Position the straw in the center between the books.

6. Using a small piece of tape, secure one of the leaves to the center of the straw.

7. Turn the straw so that the leaf is parallel to the table, then release the straw. Make note of any motion of the leaf.

8. Tape the second leaf to the straw so that the two leaves are end to end, one on either side of the straw. Then repeat step 7.

Results

With one leaf, the straw piece rotates on the dowel so that the leaf points down, perpendicular to the table. But with two leaves positioned end to end, the straw does not rotate, and the leaves remain parallel to the table.

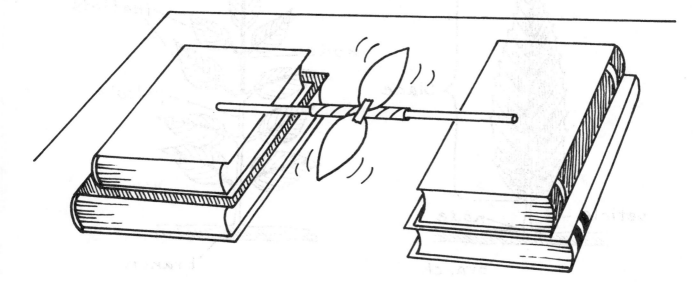

Why?

With only one leaf attached to the straw, the weight of the leaf causes the straw to rotate. With two identical leaves on either side of the straw the turning forces are balanced, and the straw doesn't rotate. As leaves develop on most broadleaf trees, they are arranged on opposite sides of the stem in opposite and alternate arrangements so there is an equal distribution of leaf weight on the stem. Some trees have **whorled** leaf arrangements, which are three or more leaves growing from one node. This ensures that the leaves will face up toward the sky and can receive more sunlight.

MORE FUN WITH LEAVES!

Observe the leaves on the trees in your neighborhood or a local park and identify the patterns in which they grow. First use the diagram here to identify the type of leaf on a tree as simple or compound, then determine whether the

pattern in which the leaves are attached is alternate, opposite or whorled. **Simple leaves** have one **blade** (flat part of a leaf) on every **petiole** (part of a plant that holds a leaf to a branch), including such trees as sycamores and elm trees. A **compound leaf** has more than one blade on a petiole, and each small blade is called a **leaflet.** Trees with compound leaves include ash and pecan trees. Use a tree field guide, such as one of those listed below, to identify the trees you observe.

BOOK LIST

Aarson, Steven M. L. *Trees.* New York: Workman Publishing Company, 1997. A Fandex Field Guide for North American Trees.

Lawrence, Eleanor and Cecilia Fitzsimons. *An Instant Guide to Trees.* New York: Gramercy Books, 1999. Nearly 200 of the most common North American trees described and illustrated in full color.

VanCleave, Janice. *Science Around the Year.* New York: Wiley, 2000. Dozens of seasonal projects and fun facts, including ones about leaves.

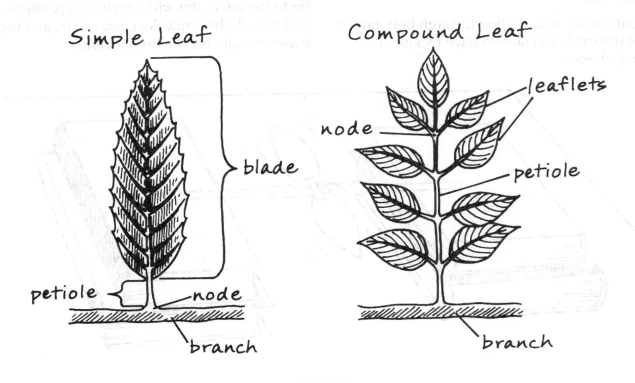

Simple Leaf — petiole, blade, node, branch

Compound Leaf — node, leaflets, petiole, branch

Deciduous Forest Animals

Animals and plants in deciduous forests have special adaptations to cope with seasonal climate changes, especially winter. Some animals survive cold winters by going into **hibernation** (dormant condition of some animals that sleep through the winter). There are degrees of hibernation ranging from deep to shallow. Animals, such as the ground squirrel that experience deep hibernation have large drops in body temperature as well as large, rapid drops in heart rate. A ground squirrel will retreat underground as winter approaches, reduce its body temperature drastically within a few hours, and become **dormant** (alive but inactive). During hibernation the squirrel's heart may beat only 10 to 20 times per minute (instead of from 200 to 300), and it may breathe only four times per minute (instead of from 100 to 200). Some animals, such as bears, badgers, raccoons, and opossums sleep in winter with little or no drop in body temperature, and their heart rate falls over a period of time. Bears of the northern forest may sleep for several months. Their heart rate may drop from 40 to 10 beats per minute and their body temperature remains normal. The bear will easily awaken if disturbed. Bears give birth during their hibernating period. Their higher body temperature during hibernation provides the energy needed for pregnancy, birth, and the nursing of young.

Some of the animals avoid the cold winters by taking part in **migrations,** which is a periodic movement of animals in response to changes in climate or food availability. Most bald eagles migrate south in the fall to warmer areas with sufficient food and return north in the spring to nest. **Fledgling** (young bird with feathers necessary for flight) bald eagles migrate before their parents. How these young birds know when and where to travel is not known. Why some return to their point of origin and others do not is another mystery.

Some animals in deciduous forests have physical adaptations that allow them to stay in the forest and stay awake during the winter. For example, large deer that live where the weather gets cold have bodies that can hold **heat** (energy that is transferred from a warm material to a cool material) for a longer time than other animals. Wolves grow a thicker coat of fur during the fall to keep them warmer in the winter. This extra hair is shed during the warmer seasons.

In areas where it snows in the winter, some animals, such as rabbits and weasels, have a change in fur color twice a year. For most of the year, the fur is brown, which blends in with the colors of the forest and helps the animal to hide from predators. But in the winter the fur is white so it blends in with the snow. The animals' fur color changes automatically, and this change is controlled by the amount of daylight there is per day. As the number of daylight hours decreases, the dark fur is shed and the new fur is white.

FUN TIME!

Purpose

To demonstrate how monarchs glide in flight.

Materials

sheet of copy paper
black marking pen
scissors
1 paper clip

Procedure

1. Lay the sheet of copy paper over the pattern shown here. Trace all the fold lines and the monarch outline. Cut out the pattern.

2. Fold the paper in half along fold line B so that the monarch outline is on the inside; then fold flaps A and C out toward the center fold.

3. Attach a paper clip under the front end, as shown.

4. Holding the paper from below (on fold line B), adjust the flaps so that they are parallel to the ground. Then throw the paper to make it glide through the air.

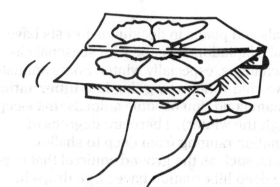

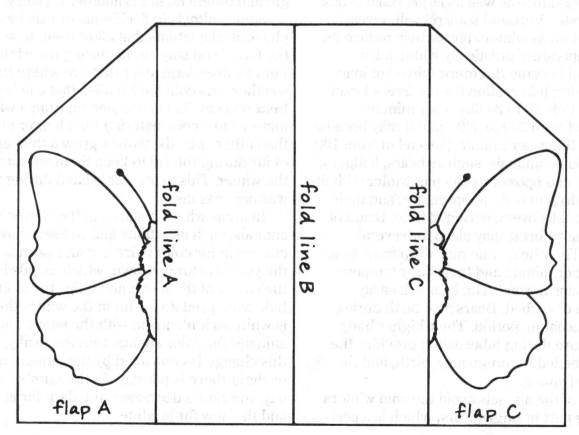

flap A   fold line A   fold line B   fold line C   flap C

Results

The paper monarch will glide through the air before landing.

Why?

Most insects in temperate climates can survive the cold winters. But monarch butterflies need more heat to stay alive, so they migrate to warmer places during the winter. Day length and temperature changes influence the migration of the monarch. Monarchs in northern regions west of the Rocky Mountains migrate to trees along the California coast. Monarchs in northern regions east of the Rocky Mountains migrate farther south to the forests high in the mountains of Mexico.

Summer monarchs have an average life span of about four to six weeks. However, the overwinter monarchs that are born in late summer live for about nine months. These butterflies migrate south during the winter and begin the return trip north as the weather begins to warm and days grow longer. They then mate and finish their lives normally.

The migrating monarchs have fat stored in their abdomens. This fat not only fuels their flight of one to three thousand miles, but it must also last until the next spring, when they migrate back north. As they migrate southward, monarchs stop to feed and actually gain weight during the trip! It is believed that to conserve energy, monarchs often hold their wings open and without moving their wings they **glide** (fly without engine power) on air currents as they travel south.

MORE FUN WITH MIGRATION!

You can help feed migrating monarchs by planting a butterfly garden. This is a garden of flowers that will supply **nectar** (sugary liquid in flowers), which is food for butterflies. Milkweeds are an important part of any butterfly garden. They not only provide nectar for many kinds of butterflies but are also the only plants the caterpillars of the monarch will accept as a food source. Milkweeds are rapidly disappearing as land is cleared for buildings. So backyard milkweed patches are becoming more important as a way of sustaining the monarch butterfly population. Find out more about which plants in your area would be suitable for planting in a butterfly garden. A local plant nursery, on-line sites, as well as butterfly books can provide information.

BOOK LIST

Pringle, Laurene. *An Extraordinary Life.* New York: Orchard Books, 1997. Introduces the life cycle, feeding habits, migration patterns, and mating habits of the monarch butterfly through the observation of one particular monarch.

Schneck, Marcus H. *Creating a Butterfly Garden: A Guide to Attracting and Identifying Butterfly Visitors.* New York: Simon and Schuster, 1994. Explains the life cycle and, migrating patterns of butterflies, as well as how to attract butterflies to a backyard garden.

VanCleave, Janice. *Animals.* New York: Wiley, 1993. Experiments about how animals keep warm and other animal experiments. Each chapter contain ideas that can be turned into award-winning science fair projects.

Leaf Colors

As summer changes into autumn in the temperate zones, the long hot days change into shorter cooler days. During autumn, the decreasing amount of sunlight causes changes in deciduous plants, most noticeably in the color of their leaves. Most leaves are green because of the presence of **chlorophyll,** which is a green **pigment** (chemical that gives a substance color) needed for the food-making process called photosynthesis. Chlorophyll is produced in response to sunlight and warm temperatures. During the growing seasons of spring and summer, chlorophyll is continually being produced and broken down, and leaves appear green. In autumn, with less sunlight and cooler temperatures, chlorophyll production slows down and eventually stops. In time all the chlorophyll is destroyed.

As old chlorophyll breaks down, other pigments, which have always been present in the leaf but have been masked or hidden by the more abundant green chlorophyll, can now be seen. These pigments include **xanthophyll,** which produces yellow colors, and **carotene,** which produces yellow-orange colors. Xanthophyll and carotene do not break down as fast as chlorophyll does, so as the amount of chlorophyll decreases or disappears, these previously masked pigments are visible for a while. But eventually all of the pigments break down, and the leaves turn brown from the presence of tannin, a brown pigment. Most red pigment in autumn leaves is due to **anthocyanin,** a red plant pigment formed as a result of cool nighttime temperatures and bright sunny days.

As the daylight decreases, most deciduous plants start growing a layer of cells across the stem beneath the petiole of each leaf. This layer is called the **abscission layer,** and the leaves are actually "cut" from the stem by this layer of cells.

FUN TIME!
Purpose

To determine the effect of sunlight on the color of leaves.

Materials

deciduous tree or bush with large, dark green leaves
3-by-5-inch (7.5-by-12.5-cm) index card
scissors
paper hole punch
4 paper clips
transparent tape

Procedure

1. With adult approval, select 4 or more leaves of equal size on the plant that will be used in this experiment. The leaves should all receive equal amounts of sunlight and *remain on the plant* during the experiment.

2. Fold the index card in half two times, placing the long sides together for each fold.

3. Unfold the card and cut along each of the three folds, forming four strips.

4. Fold one of the strips in half, placing the short ends together.

5. Using the paper hole punch, punch two holes in the folded strip, cutting through both layers. Then slip this strip around one of the selected leaves. Secure the ends of the strip with a paper clip.

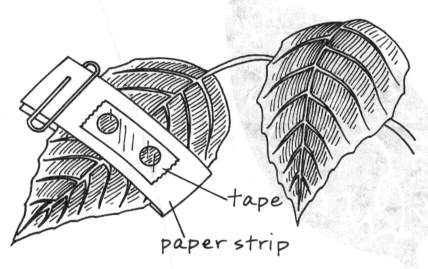

tape

paper strip

6. Cover the holes in the paper strip on the top and underside of the leaf with transparent tape.

7. Repeat steps 4 through 6, using the three remaining paper strips.

8. Remove the paper strips after 7 or more days and observe the color of the leaves.

Results

In areas covered by the paper strip, the leaves change from dark green to pale green to yellow. The areas not covered by the strip, as well as those beneath the holes cut in the card, do not noticeably change color.

Why?

Light is necessary for a plant to produce chlorophyll. During the natural aging process of plants, chlorophyll molecules break down and are replaced. But without light, when the chlorophyll breaks down, it is not replaced. When the chlorophyll is no longer present, other pigments in the leaf that were masked by the color of chlorophyll can now be seen. In this experiment, the paper strip blocked the sunlight, and in time, the chlorophyll present in the leaf broke down and the yellow pigment it masked became visible. The fact that the part of the leaves under the holes covered with **transparent** (allows light to pass through) tape did not turn yellow shows that covering the leaf did not cause the color change.

This same color-changing process occurs in deciduous leaves in the autumn when they no longer produce new chlorophyll. The yellow and orange pigments in the leaves do not break down as fast as chlorophyll does, so they are seen only when the green chlorophyll is gone.

MORE FUN WITH LEAVES!

A leaf's yellow color pigments are masked by the presence of green chlorophyll. Try this activity to make leaf art by covering and then uncovering pigments. Draw a leaf shape on a piece of white copy paper. Use a yellow marker to color the leaf. Using a dark green crayon, color over the yellow with a thick layer of green. Open one end of a paper clip and use the tip of the paper clip to draw designs in the colored leaf. Press down on the clip only hard enough so that it scratches away the green layer and exposes the yellow marker layer beneath.

BOOK LIST

Burton, Jane, and Kid Tailor. *The Nature and Science of Leaves.* Milwaukee: Gareth Stevens Publishing, 1997. Information about leaves, including how they change color.

Johnson, Sylvia. *How Leaves Change.* Minneapolis: Lerner Publications Company, 1986. Information about deciduous leaves, including how they change colors.

VanCleave, Janice. *Plants.* New York: Wiley, 1997. Experiments about plants, including some about color changes in leaves. Each chapter contains ideas that can be turned into award-winning science fair projects.

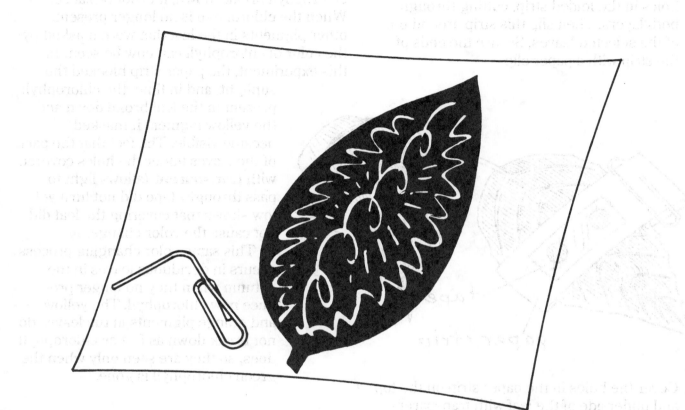

CONIFEROUS FORESTS

A **coniferous forest** is a biome characterized by conifers such as pine, fir, and spruce trees which are generally evergreen and usually have needle-shaped leaves. This type of forest is found mainly in the Northern Hemisphere north of the temperate forests, as well as at high elevations on mountains above deciduous forests. There are two types of coniferous forests, the open woodlands, with widely spaced trees, and dense forest, with trees that grow close together. Other names for coniferous forests are **boreal forest** and **taiga.**

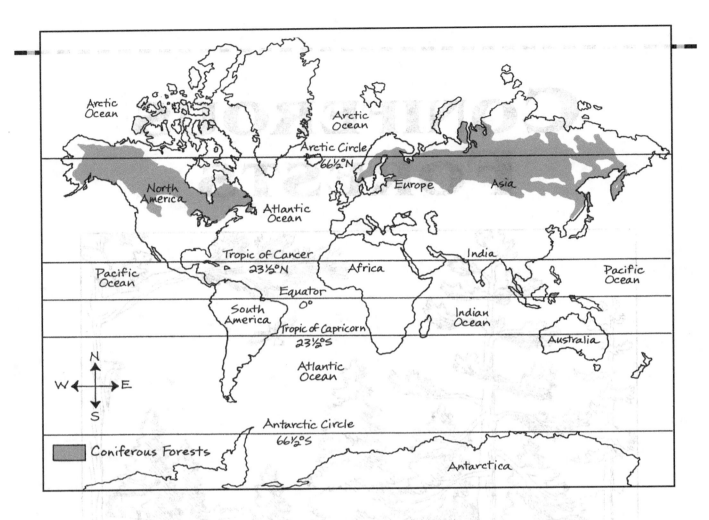

Arctic
Ocean

Arctic
Ocean

Arctic Circle
66½°N

North
America

Europe   Asia

Atlantic
Ocean

India

Tropic of Cancer
23½°N   Africa

Pacific
Ocean

Pacific
Ocean

Equator
0°

South
America

Indian
Ocean

Tropic of Capricorn
23½°S

Australia

Atlantic
Ocean

N
W ← → E
S

Antarctic Circle
66½°S

Coniferous Forests

Antarctica

Northern coniferous forests form an irregular band about 800 to 900 miles (1,280 to 1,440 km) wide across the northern (between 50°N and 60°N) latitudes of land masses in the Northern Hemisphere. The border of the coniferous forests to the north of these latitudes, as well as at higher altitudes, is called the **timberline** (the line in northern latitudes and on mountains above which no trees grow).

Winters in the coniferous forests are bitterly cold with an average low of –22°F (–30°C), and last about eight or nine months. However, the coniferous forests make up the largest land

biome, and temperatures can vary from one place to another. Generally, the farther north or the higher the elevation of this biome, the colder the region is. Growing seasons last only about three to four months, and summers average highs of 70°F (21°C). Precipitation is evenly distributed throughout the year with a yearly average of 15 to 40 inches (37.5 to 100 cm). The humidity is usually high.

In this section, you'll investigate the types of trees, plant adaptation, and food chains in coniferous forests.

Conifers

Gymnosperms are seed plants that do not produce flowers or fruit. Instead, most of these plants produce cones or conelike structures. Cone-bearing gymnosperms are called conifers. Conifers have "naked seeds," which means the seeds are not surrounded by the tissue of a fruit as angiosperm (flowering plants) seeds are. Instead, the seeds of conifers are stored inside cones, except for the yew and the ginko, which produce a berrylike structure that covers their seeds. Most conifers are evergreen trees that have small needle-shaped leaves.

There are about 600 conifer species, including pines, firs, spruces, cedars, junipers, and yew. Conifers have two types of cones. One is a small cone, called the **pollen cone,** which contains **pollen** (tiny capsules that contain the male reproductive cells, called **sperm**). The other is a **seed cone,** which contains seeds. A seed is formed as a result of **sexual reproduction,** which is the union of a sperm and **egg** (female reproductive cell) in the seed cone. Pollen cones of pine trees generally form in groups at the tip of a branch, and seed cones generally form as a single cone away from the tip of a branch. The seed is formed when wind blows pollen grains from the pollen cones to the seed cones. It takes two or more years for the seeds to develop completely. During the seed-development stage, the cone grows larger, and the scales close tightly to protect the seeds. When the seeds are completely developed, the scales of the pinecones open slightly and the seeds fall to the ground.

Some conifers are shrubs but most are tall, straight trees with branches growing at a 90-degree angle or horizontally from the tree trunk. Conifers are among the largest trees in the world. The giant sequoia in central California reaches heights of between about 3,000 and 8,000 feet (about 900 and 2,400 m). These giants have diameters of up to 30 feet (9 m), with bark thicknesses of up to 24 inches (60 cm). Buttresses at the base of the sequoia trunk form a natural support structure to these tall trees. Some giant sequoias are more than 2,000 years old.

FUN TIME!

Purpose

To locate the seeds of pinecones.

Materials

several sheets of newspaper
1 old washcloth
2 to 3 small, developed pinecones with
   tightly closed scales

Procedure

1. Spread the newspaper on a table.

2. Wrap the washcloth around both ends of one of the pinecones. The cloth prevents the cone from damaging your hands.

3. Holding a washcloth-covered end in each hand, twist the pinecone back and forth several times to loosen its scales.

4. While holding the base of the cone with the cloth in one hand, use your other hand to pull out several scales near the tip of the pinecone.

5. Look for two seeds on the inside of each scale, as shown. If you do not find seeds, repeat steps 2 to 4 with another pinecone. *Note: Loose-scaled pinecones may have lost their seeds.*

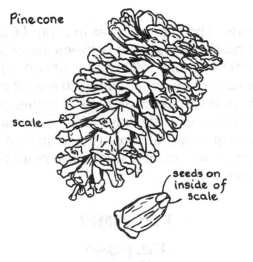

Pinecone

scale

seeds on inside of scale

Results

Two seeds, each attached to a paperlike wing, are found on the inside of each scale of the pinecone.

Why?

Pine trees are conifers with small green needle-shaped leaves. Conifers got their name because they make their seeds in cones, instead of producing them from flowers. Pinecones are the seed cones of a pine tree. Seed cones are able to protect the seed inside from changes in temperature. When the seeds have completely developed, the scales of pinecones open slightly and the seeds fall to the ground or are blown out by the wind.

MORE FUN WITH CONIFERS!

Pinecones are **hygroscopic** (able to **absorb** [take in] water from the air). When pinecones' scales absorb water, they swell and close. Drying allows the scales to separate. You can observe pinecones to tell whether the air is humid or dry. Test the humidity of the air in your home by placing four or more pinecones in two different containers. Small baskets will make the pinecone arrangement an attractive addition to the room. Use mature pinecones, the largest cones produced by the tree. Set the baskets in different rooms of the house, such as the bathroom and a bedroom. Over a period of seven or more days, compare the difference in the scales on the pinecones in each room. If there is no change, soak the cones from one basket in a bowl of water. After 30 minutes or more, remove the cones and compare their scales with the dry cones to determine if the air in your home is dry or humid. Remember that pinecones absorb water from the air, and humid air contains more water than dry air.

BOOK LIST

Braithwaite, Althea. *Trees and Leaves.* New York: Troll Associates, 1990. Information and colored diagrams about leaves and trees, including conifers.

NatureScope: *Trees Are Terrific!* Washington, D.C.: National Wildlife Federation, 1992. Information about trees, including information and diagrams about conifers as well as indoor and outdoor activities.

VanCleave, Janice. *Plants.* New York: Wiley, 1997. Experiments about plants, including some about conifers. Each chapter contains ideas that can be turned into award-winning science fair projects.

Adaptations of Coniferous Plants

Though most of the trees in coniferous forests are evergreens, there are also some deciduous trees, such as aspen and birch. Unlike the tropical forest, where there is a mixture of many different kinds of trees, coniferous forests have many trees but of only a few kinds. Underneath the trees is a spotty layer of shrubs. Mosses and lichens grow on the forest floor as well as on the tree trunks and branches.

Since most water in coniferous forests is frozen during the winter, it is not available for plant roots to absorb it. Many evergreen trees, much like desert plants, are adapted to the scarce water supply because they have small leaves with a limited surface area and a waxy coating, which helps hold water in. Falling snow can collect on the limbs of trees with round or square crowns, causing the limbs to break. But the triangular shape of the crown of these trees and the needlelike shape of their leaves lets conifers more easily shed heavy snow buildups.

Adaptation is a structure or behavior that helps an organism survive in its **environment** (all the living and nonliving surroundings of an organism). One adaptation by coniferous plants to a short growing season in coniferous forests is their retention of leaves, which allows them to start photosynthesis as soon as temperatures permit in the spring, instead of having to spend time growing leaves. Another adaptation is the dark color of their leaves, which helps to absorb heat from sunlight.

FUN TIME!

Purpose

To demonstrate how the shape of a tree affects its ability to collect snow.

Materials

newspaper
two 6-by-10-inch (15-by-25-cm) pieces of
 poster board
transparent tape
spoon
flour

Procedure

1. Unfold the newspaper and lay it on a table.

2. Fold one of the poster board pieces in half by placing the short sides together.

3. Partially unfold the folded poster board, creating a tent shape.

4. Stand the tent-shaped poster board on the newspaper and secure it to the newspaper with tape.

5. Tape one of the short ends of the other piece of poster board to the newspaper.

6. Bend this poster board to form a dome shape, then tape the other short end of this poster board to the newspaper.

7. Using the spoon, sprinkle 4 or more spoons of flour over the top of the tent-shaped structure. Observe how the flour builds up on the structure.

8. Repeat procedure 7, but use the dome-shaped structure.

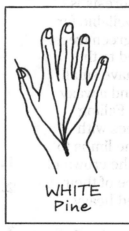

Results

The tent-shaped structure held little to no flour, while most or all of the flour built up on the dome-shaped structure.

Why?

The tent shape, like the triangular shape of some conifers, doesn't provide a large surface area. Thus like the flour in this experiment, snow tends to slide off the leaves and branches. Though little flour built up on the tent-shaped poster board in the experiment, real triangular-shaped conifer trees have more surface area, so some buildup of snow does occur and some trees do collect more snow than others. At times the weight of the snow will cause tree limbs to break. This opens areas so that sunlight can reach the forest floor and more plants can grow there.

MORE FUN WITH TREES!

Pine trees have long thin needles that are grouped in clusters. Each cluster contains a specific number of needles, depending on the type of tree. Pines are divided into two groups, based on the hardness of their wood. The soft pines have needles in bundles of five. White pine is a well-known soft pine. The hard pines, such as red pine and pitch pine, have needles in bundles of two or three. Both soft and hard pine wood is used for lumber. Look at the needles from a pine tree. Count the needles in one cluster. Use the diagram to determine if the wood of the pine tree that the needles came from is soft or hard.

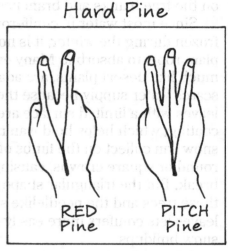

Soft Pine — WHITE Pine

Hard Pine — RED Pine, PITCH Pine

BOOK LIST

NatureScope: *Trees Are Terrific!* Washington, D.C.: National Wildlife Federation, 1992. Information as well as indoor and outdoor activities about trees, including those in coniferous forests.

VanCleave, Janice. *Ecology for Every Kid.* New York: Wiley, 1996. Fun, simple ecology experiments, including information about coniferous forests.

12

Food Chains

A **food chain** is a model that shows how a group of organisms are linked together in the order in which they feed on one another. Different food chains contain different organisms, but they all show how food moves from one organism to another, giving energy to the organism eating the food. For example, a simple coniferous forest food chain might be a leaf being eaten by a caterpillar, which is eaten by a small bird such as a jay, which is eaten by a cat, such as a lynx.

The primary source of energy for a food chain comes from the Sun. Plants use the Sun's energy to produce food by photosynthesis. Thus plants are called **producers** (organisms in a food chain that can produce their own food). Animals are called **consumers** (organisms that cannot produce their own food, so they have to feed on other organisms).

Organisms may be grouped according to how they acquire their food, and their role in the flow of energy through a food chain called a **trophic level** (feeding level). The first trophic level consists of **primary producers,** which are plants that provide food for primary consumers. **Primary consumers** are **herbivores** (animals that eat plants), which belong to the second trophic level. Primary consumers are eaten by **secondary consumers,** which are **carnivores** (flesh-eating animals). Secondary consumers are eaten by **tertiary consumers,** and so on. The levels above the primary consumer are numbered sequentially, with the final carnivore in the top level, called the **ultimate consumer** or **top carnivore.** As the trophic levels rise, the **predators** (animals that kill and eat other animals) become fewer,

larger, fiercer, and more agile. **Omnivores** (animals that eat both plants and animals) generally belong to the second and third trophic levels.

In time all organisms, both plants and animals, die and are consumed by **decomposers** (organisms, such as bacteria and fungi, that get their nutrients by breaking down the chemicals in waste and dead organisms). The nutrients that come from this decomposition become part of the soil which is then reused by new plants back at the start of the food chain.

There are usually links between different food chains in an **ecosystem** (a certain place and the living and nonliving things found there). When all the possible interconnections are mapped out for an ecosystem, a **food web** (all the possible food patterns in an ecosystem) is formed. A simple food web is shown in the diagram. A complete food web for a coniferous forest or any ecosystem would contain all possible feeding transfers.

A **food pyramid** is a pyramid-shaped model that compares the organisms in each trophic level of a food chain. The number of organisms in each level decreases from the bottom to the top, because each organism must eat more of the organisms in the level beneath it to get enough energy to live.

FUN TIME!
Purpose

To construct a food pyramid.

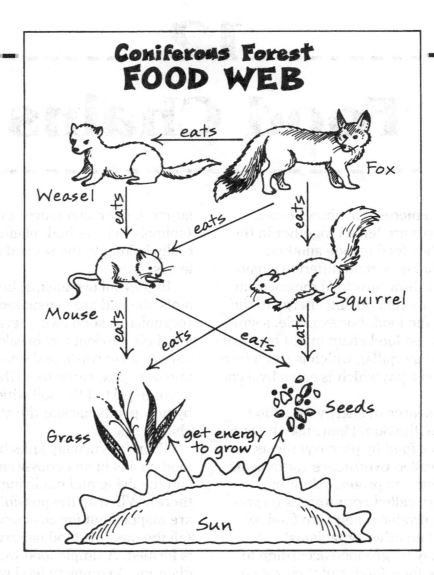

Coniferous Forest FOOD WEB

Weasel

Fox

eats

eats

eats

eats

Mouse

Squirrel

eats

eats

eats

eats

Grass

get energy to grow

Seeds

Sun

Materials

8-inch (20-cm) square piece of white copy
   paper
marking pen
ruler
scissors
transparent tape

Procedure

1. Fold the paper diagonally. Unfold the
   paper and refold it the opposite way.
   Unfold the paper. Four triangles will be
   formed.

2. Use the pen and ruler to draw three lines
   across three of the triangles on the paper,
   dividing each triangle into four parts.

3. From top to bottom, label the four parts of
   one triangle: Tertiary Consumer,
   Secondary Consumer, Primary Consumer,
   Producer.

4. From top to bottom, label the four parts of a
   second triangle, Gray Wolf, Red Fox,
   Squirrel, Tree Seeds.

5. In the four parts of the remaining triangle,
   draw a picture of each item represented in
   step 3.

6. Cut along a fold line between the third triangle and the remaining unmarked fourth triangle.

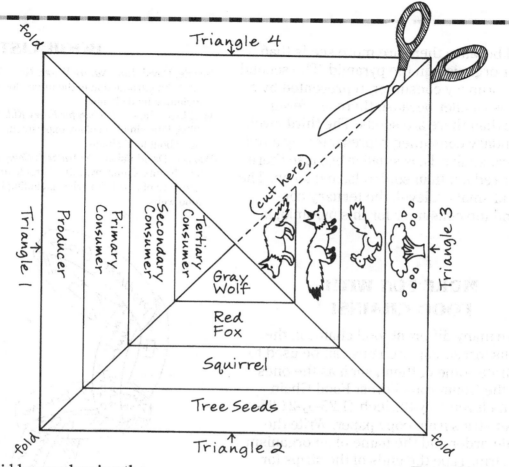

Triangle 4

fold

Triangle 1

Producer

Primary Consumer

Secondary Consumer

Tertiary Consumer

(cut here)

Triangle 3

Gray Wolf

Red Fox

Squirrel

Tree Seeds

fold

fold

Triangle 2

7. Form a pyramid by overlapping the unmarked triangle with triangle 3. Secure with tape.

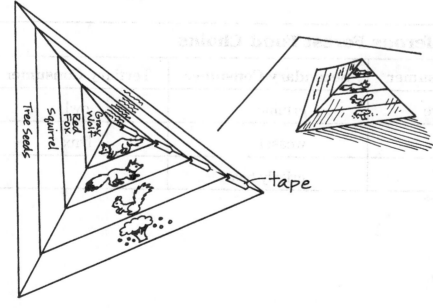

Tree Seeds

Squirrel

Red Fox

Gray Wolf

tape

Results

You made a coniferous forest food pyramid.

Why?

There are four levels in the food pyramid made in this investigation. There are rarely more than five levels in any pyramid model. The pyramid in this experiment is called a **pyramid of number,** which is a food pyramid in which the numbers of organisms decrease as you move up the food chain from the producer to the top consumer. The tree seeds are the first level, the producer. The pyramid is widest at this level because there are more seeds than any other organism in the pyramid. The second level, the primary consumer, represented by a squirrel, is smaller because there are fewer squirrels than there are seeds. The third level, the secondary consumer, represented by a red fox that eat squirrels, is smaller because there are fewer red fox than squirrels, and so on. The fourth and smallest level, the tertiary consumer and top consumer for this pyramid, is the wolf.

MORE FUN WITH FOOD CHAINS!

There are many different food chains in the coniferous forest. Paper chains can be used to demonstrate some of them, such as the ones listed in the Coniferous Forest Food Chain table. Cut eleven 1-by-8½-inch (1.25-by-21.25-cm) paper strips from copy paper. Write the food chain order and the name of an organism on each strip. Tape the ends of the strips for the producers together. Then form links by connecting the other strips in order, as shown.

BOOK LIST

Burnie, David. *How Nature Works.* New York: Reader's Digest, 1991. An introduction to the miraculous world of nature, including food chains.

VanCleave, Janice. *Ecology for Every Kid.* New York: Wiley, 1996. Fun, simple ecology experiments, including information about food chains.

Wallace, David Rains. *The Walker's Companion.* San Francisco: The Nature Company, 1995. A guide to the fascinating fauna and flora of North America, including how they relate in food webs.

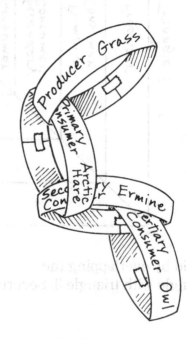

Coniferous Forest Food Chains			
Producer	**Primary Consumer**	**Secondary Consumer**	**Tertiary Consumer**
grass	Arctic hare	ermine	owl
grass	lemming	weasel	lynx
water plants	beaver	grizzly bear	

II

GRASSLANDS

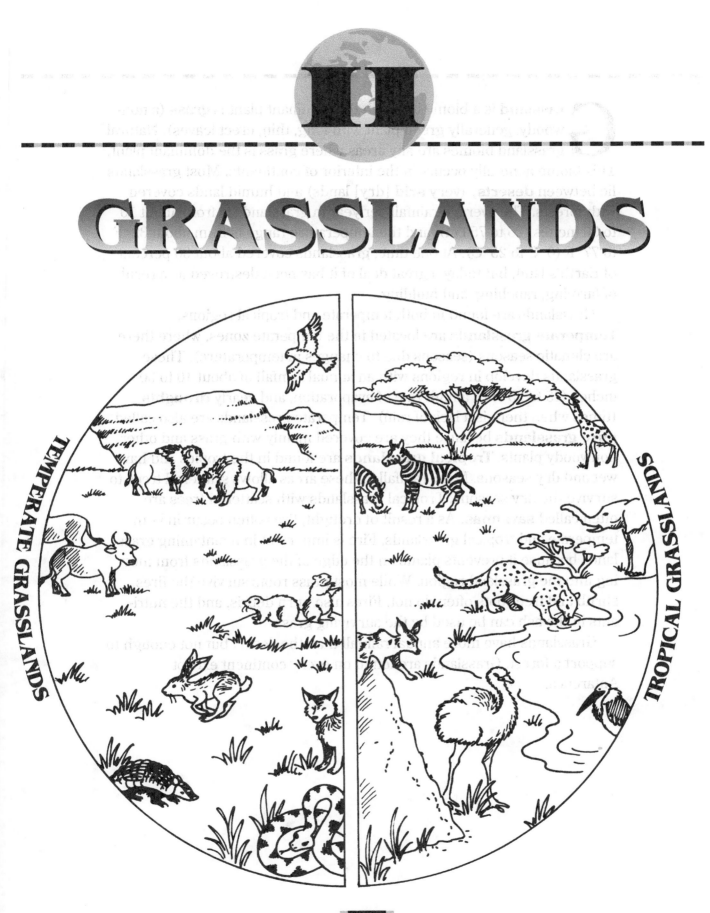

TEMPERATE GRASSLANDS

TROPICAL GRASSLANDS

Grassland is a biome in which the dominant plant is **grass** (a nonwoody, generally green plant with long, thin, erect leaves). Natural grassland biomes are any areas where grass is the dominant plant. This biome generally occurs in the interior of continents. Most grasslands lie between **deserts,** (very **arid** [dry] lands) and humid lands covered with forests. The average rainfall per year in grasslands is from about 10 to 30 inches (25 to 75 cm), and the temperature range is from about 32°F to 77°F (0°C to 25°C). At one time, grasslands covered about 30 percent of Earth's land, but today a great deal of it has been destroyed as a result of farming, ranching, and building.

Grasslands are found in both temperate and tropical regions. **Temperate grasslands** are located in the temperate zones, where there are climatic seasons (seasons due to changes in temperature). These grasslands develop in regions with an annual rainfall of about 10 to 30 inches (25 to 75 cm), a high rate of evaporation, and yearly **droughts** (times when there is a lack of rain). Temperate grasslands are also called **pure grasslands** because they are covered mainly with grass and other nonwoody plants. **Tropical grasslands** are found in the tropics and have wet and dry seasons. More rainfall in these areas allows scattered trees to survive the dry seasons. Tropical grasslands with scattered trees are often called **savannas.** As a result of drought, fires often occur in both temperate and tropical grasslands. Fire is important in maintaining grasslands because it prevents plants on the edge of the grasslands from moving into the grassland region. While most grass roots survive the fires, shrub and tree roots often do not. Fires also burn debris, and the nutrients in the ash can be used by the surviving grass.

Grasslands have more annual rainfall than the desert but not enough to support a forest. Grasslands are found on every continent except Antarctica.

TEMPERATE GRASSLANDS

Temperate grasslands are regions in the temperate zones in which grass is the dominant plant. There are basically no trees and few to no shrubs in these areas. Temperate grasslands have different names in different parts of the world, such as **prairies** in North America, **pampas** of Argentina, **campos** of Uruguay and Brazil, **veldts** of South Africa, **steppes** of Central Eurasia, and **rangelands** of Australia and New Zealand.

Temperate grasslands have hot summers and cold winters with a moderate annual

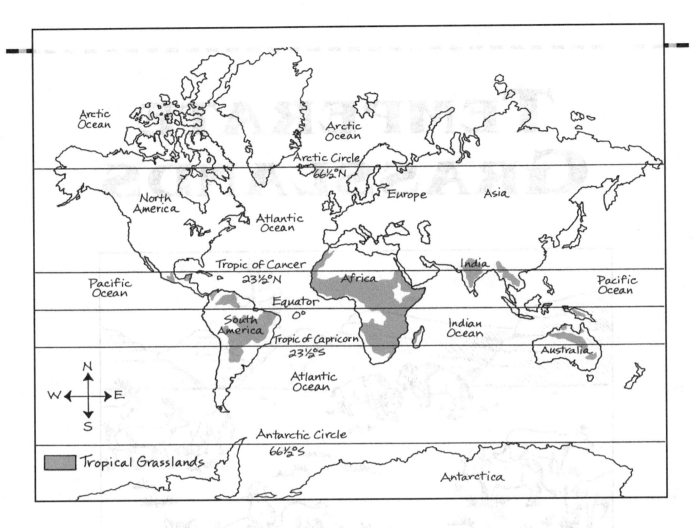

Tropical Grasslands

rainfall of about 10 to 30 inches (25 to 75 cm). These regions have a high rate of evaporation. The key to an area remaining a natural grassland is occasional fires and droughts, which prevent woody shrubs and trees from growing. The amount of annual rainfall influences the height of grassland vegetation. Taller grasses are found in wetter regions. The seasonal droughts, occasional fires, and grazing by large mammals all prevent woody shrubs and trees

from invading and becoming established. However a few trees, such as cottonwoods, oaks, and willows, grow in river valleys, and some nonwoody plants, specifically a few hundred species of flowers, grow among the grasses.

In this section, you'll determine the effect of grass on soil erosion, learn about the characteristics of prairie grasses, and investigate some of the animals in temperate grasslands.

Grasses

Grass is a common name for one of the largest groups of flowering plants. Unlike the flowers of many plants, grass flowers do not have large, colorful petals. But like all flowers, grass flowers are part of the seed production of the plant.

There are about 9,000 different kinds of grasses. Grasses are more widely distributed around Earth than any other group of flowering plants. Some kind of grass is found on almost all terrestrial biomes, and grasses are the only flowering plants to grow on the cold, icy Antarctic continent. Grasses are found in forests, deserts, and tundras, but grasses are most abundant in the open areas of grasslands.

Grasses are usually green because they contain a green-colored substance called chlorophyll (green pigment). Through a process called photosynthesis, this material helps change sunlight into energy. Grasses are the primary source of food for wild grazing animals found in grasslands.

Grasslands have some protection from wind and water **erosion** (the process by which materials of Earth's surface are broken down and carried away by natural agents, such as wind and water) because of their grass covering. Grasses have **fibrous roots,** which are roots that have no main section but spread out into the soil in all directions. Fibrous roots are thin and form a tangled mass in shallow soil. This mass helps to hold the soil together, so wind and water do not easily erode the soil.

Besides having fibrous roots, most grasses are **herbaceous** (nonwoody) plants, which means they have stems that are relatively soft. The leaves of grasses are attached along the soft stem at points called nodes. Each leaf is made of two parts: the blade and the sheath. The blade (flat part of a leaf) is usually long and narrow, with parallel veins. The leaf blade has growth tissue near the node on the stem and grows here rather than at the tip. This is why its tip can be cut and it will continue to grow. The **sheath,** which supports the blade, wraps partially around the base of the blade and is open at least part of the way down.

Some grasses have **stolons** (horizontal stems that grow above ground), which are commonly called **runners.** Other grasses have horizontal stems that grow below ground called **rhizomes.** New grass plants grow from stolons and rhizomes.

FUN TIME!

Purpose

To determine how grass affects soil erosion.

Materials

six 12-ounce (360-mL) paper cups

dirt (potting soil will work)

marker

tap water

pencil

two 6-by-12-inch (15-by-30-cm) pieces of
    corrugated cardboard

shallow baking pan (a plastic serving tray
    will work)

grass clippings

Procedure

1. Fill two of the paper cups with dirt or potting soil.

2. Fill three of the paper cups with water.

3. Use the pencil to make 6 small holes in the bottom of one of the remaining paper cups. Use the marker to label this cup A.

4. Place the baking pan on an outdoor table or on the ground. Position the piece of cardboard in the baking pan so that one of the narrow ends of the cardboard is on the edge of the pan.

5. Pour one of the cups of dirt on the cardboard and spread it into a thin layer.

6. Hold the paper cup with the holes (cup A) about 6 inches (15 cm) above the dirt on the cardboard. While in this position pour water from one of the cups into cup A. Move cup A back and forth across the dirt so that the water falls on it like rain.

7. When the water has stopped running off the dirt-covered cardboard, observe the amount of dirt in the pan.

8. Remove the cardboard and use a second cup of water to wash the dirt out of the pan.

9. Repeat steps 4 and 5, covering the cardboard with the other cup of dirt.

10. Using your hands, tear off enough blades of grass to cover the dirt on the cardboard with a thick layer of the grass clippings.

11. Repeat steps 6 and 7.

Results

Dirt is washed off the cardboard into the pan. More dirt is washed away from the uncovered dirt layer than from the layer of dirt with grass covering it.

Why?

Rain, like the falling water from the cup in this experiment, erodes soil by moving it from one place to another. When the soil is covered, even with a layer of loose grass clippings, some of the water runs over the surface covering, and less soil is eroded. Much like the grass clippings in this experiment, grass blades provide a protective covering for soil, but the grass roots provide even more protection from erosion because they hold the soil together.

MORE FUN WITH GRASS!

Identify the different parts of grass. With adult permission, dig up a clump of grass and dip the roots in a bucket of water to rinse off any clinging dirt. Use the diagram shown to identify the different parts of the grass. If there is a horizontal stem, determine if it is a stolon (above-ground stem) or a rhizome (below-ground stem).

BOOK LIST

Pope, Joyce. *Plants and Flowers.* Mahwah, N.J.: Troll Associates, 1994. Interesting facts about wild plants, including grass.

Knope, Jim. *Natural Gardening.* New York: Time Life Books, 1995. A guide showing how to improve the ecology of where you live by learning about animals and plants, including grasses.

VanCleave, Janice. *Ecology for Every Kid.* New York: Wiley, 1996. Fun, simple ecology experiments, including information about grass.

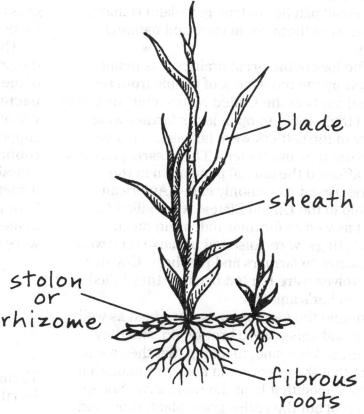

Prairie Grasses

The temperate grasslands in North America are called prairies. At one time, prairies were the largest biomes in North America. Today only small patches of true grassland remain, and most of them are in state and national parks.

The loss of the great prairies was mainly caused by the movement of people from the settled lands of the United States after the Civil War (1861–1865) to open lands farther west. Many of the settlers were farmers, but some were hunters and traders. These early pioneers first affected the animal population in the prairie. Bison (commonly called American Buffalo in the United States) were killed for sport as well as for their hides and meat. Prairie dogs were poisoned because they were a nuisance to farmers and ranchers. Coyotes and wolves were hunted because they killed the rancher's animals.

In time the natural grass was killed as well. Cattle and sheep were brought in, and they overgrazed the land, meaning that they ate so much that the grass could not grow enough to produce food that kept the roots alive. Sheep often pull out the entire grass plant, roots and all. Farmers also helped destroy the grassland by replacing the natural grasses with crops such as wheat and corn.

When the prairie grassland was present, two basic factors kept grasses as the dominant plant. One was the occasional natural fires, caused by lightning. Any shrubs or trees that might have started growing in the area were burned. While the grass also burned, it was able to regrow from underground roots, unlike the shrubs and trees. Fires also cleared the ground of matted grasses that restricted new grass growth. The nutrients in the burned grass were added to the soil, making it fertile for new grass to grow in.

The second factor keeping other plants off the prairies were bison. The constant trampling of the ground by these heavy animals **compacted** (squeezed together) the soil so that water could not penetrate deeply enough to support the roots of trees or shrubs. Bison also rubbed against the trees on the edge of the grasslands. This helped the bison to shed their winter fur, but the rubbing also stripped the bark from some of the trees, causing the trees to die. Thus the boundaries of the grasslands were maintained.

FUN TIME!

Purpose

To make a model of the height of grasses in the North American prairie.

Materials

ruler

pen

1 sheet of 8½-by-11-inch (21.25-by-27.5 cm) white copy paper

green crayon

scissors

transparent tape

Procedure

1. Use the ruler and pen to draw a line across the short side of the paper and indented ½ inch (1.25 cm) from the edge.

2. Draw two more lines, 4 inches (10 cm) apart and parallel to the first line.

3. Draw grass in the small section, as shown, and color it.

4. In the center section, about 1 inch (2.5 cm) from the bottom, draw a 3-by-⅛-inch (7.5-by-0.3-cm) "cut out," as shown. Cut out this section.

5. In the third section, 1 inch (2.5 cm) up from the bottom, draw a 2-by-6-inch (5-by-15-cm) "cut out," as shown. Cut out this section.

6. Label the third section Prairie Grasses.

7. Label the left side of the cutout areas in section three Average Yearly Rainfall and the right side Grass Height, as shown.

8. Make a mark even with the top and on both sides of the cutout areas. Make two additional sets of marks, one 2.5 inches (6.25 cm) from the top mark and the other 5 inches (12.5 cm) from the top mark.

9. Starting at the top mark on the left of the opening, label the average yearly rainfall: High, Med, Low.

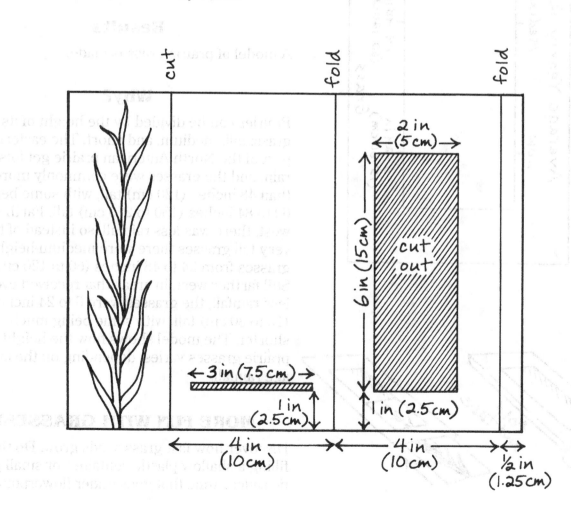

10. Starting at the top mark on the left, label the grass height: 48 in. (120 cm), 24–48 in. (60–120 cm), 6–24 in. (15–60 cm).

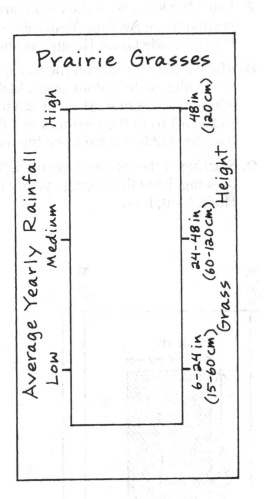

11. Cut along the indicated line to separate the grass strip from the other sections.

12. Score each fold line by laying the ruler along each of the fold lines, then trace the lines with the pen.

13. Fold the paper along fold line 1, then along fold line 2, and secure the folded sections together with tape.

14. Insert the top end of the grass strip in the grass strip slot so that the colored side of the strip is visible through the opening in the front of the model.

15. Move the grass strip up and down to model the different heights of grass.

Results

A model of prairie grass is made.

Why?

Prairies can be divided by the height of its grass: tall, medium, and short. The eastern part of the North American prairie got lots of rain, and the grasses were commonly more than 48 inches (120 cm) tall, with some being 60 to 84 inches (150 to 210 cm) tall. Farther west, there was less rainfall, so instead of the very tall grasses there were medium-height grasses from 24 to 48 inches (60 to 120 cm) tall. Still farther west, in areas that received even less rainfall, the grasses were 6 to 24 inches (15 to 30 cm) tall, with some being much shorter. The model shows how the height of prairie grasses varies, depending on the average rainfall.

MORE FUN WITH GRASSES!

Discover how fast grass seeds grow. Do this by filling a shallow plastic container or small plastic saucer (one that goes under flowerpots) about three-fourths full with potting soil. Smooth the surface of the soil, then use a pencil to dig out trenches about ¼ inch (0.63 cm) deep in the shape of your initial. Sprinkle grass seeds, such as rye grass, in the trenches. Cover the trenches with soil. Use a spray bottle to spray the surface of the soil with water. Moisten the soil, but do not make it dripping wet. Spray the surface of the soil every day or as often as necessary to keep it moist. When the seeds sprout, your garden will have grass growing in the shape of your initial.

BOOK LIST

Fredricks, Anthony D. *Simple Nature Experiments with Everyday Materials.* New York: Sterling Publishing Co., 1995. Facts, illustrations, and creative projects about soil and other nature topics.

VanCleave, Janice. *Ecology for Every Kid.* New York: Wiley, 1996. Fun, simple ecology experiments, including information about grasslands.

Prairie Animals

The animals that live in prairies have adapted to a semidry, windy environment with very few to no trees or shrubs. They can also withstand a great range in temperature, from well below freezing in the winter to hot in the summer. Many animals live in prairies, ranging from insects, such as bees, grasshoppers, and beetles, and small mammals, such as rats, mice, ground squirrels, prairie dogs, coyotes, wolves, and fox, to large mammals, such as antelopes, elk, deer, and at one time large herds of bison. A number of birds live in the prairies, including prairie chickens, hawks and owls. Other animals, including snakes, also make their home in prairies.

While many of these animals are found in other biomes, prairie chickens and prairie dogs are generally found only in short-grass prairies. The prairie chicken is not a chicken but is actually a relative of the ringed-necked pheasant. While most birds perch and nest in trees, the prairie chicken is a ground dweller, even though it can fly. These birds are an **endangered species,** which is an organism that is in danger of **extinction** (the dying off of all individuals of a species). Hunting and changes in habitat are some of the things that cause an organism to become extinct.

Prairie dogs are not dogs but are actually similar to ground squirrels. These animals live in large groups and burrow into the ground, sometimes forming miles of underground tunnels. They were such an oddity to the explorers Lewis and Clark that they sent a prairie dog to President Thomas Jefferson during their expedition in the prairies of North America.

Prairie dogs are hunted by many animals, including wolves, dogs, coyotes, bobcats, foxes, and some people. A prairie dog's best defense is to retreat into a burrow.

In the prairie and other grasslands, grass is the primary producer for most food chains. Consumers in each food chain have special adaptations in order to survive. For example, the fur on the backs of wolves is in three overlapping layers, starting at the neck. When it rains, water runs off these layers. This adaptation is particularly useful to the wolf because the landscape provides little to no natural shelter for prairie animals during rain or other stormy weather. Wolves and some other animals, such as deer and fox, have large ears that can turn, which aids in hearing and locating sounds. Again, prairies do not have many places for large animals to hide, so having good hearing helps them to be aware of approaching predators.

FUN TIME!

Purpose

To determine how ear size can help an animal escape a predator.

Materials

scissors
9-ounce (270-mL) or larger paper cup
ticking watch or clock

Procedure

1. Use the scissors to cut the bottom out of the paper cup.

2. With your left hand, hold the watch near your left ear.

3. Move the watch away from your ear until you can barely hear it tick. Note the distance of the watch from your ear.

4. Using the other hand, hold the small end of the paper cup over the ear aimed at the watch.

5. Hold the watch at the end of the paper cup over your ear.

6. Repeat step 3 and compare the difference between the distances the watch can be heard with and without the cup.

Results

When you used the paper cup, you were able to hear the ticking of the watch at a greater distance.

Why?

The sound of the ticking watch spreads out from the watch much like water waves spread over the surface of water in which a pebble has been dropped. Your **external ear** (part of the ear on the outside of your head) collects some of this sound. The cup extending from your ear increases the amount of sound that is collected, so the ticking can be heard when the watch is held at a greater distance. Larger external ears on animals help them hear predators approaching from a distance and gives them more time to escape.

MORE FUN WITH HEARING!

Wolves, deer, fox, and other animals are also able to move their ears. This allows them to locate the source of a sound by moving only their ears while keeping their bodies still, so they are less likely to attract attention. See how animals turning their ears helps locate sounds. First stand or sit in the center of a room and ask four or more helpers to stand about 3 feet (0.9 m) from you. You want to have a helper on each side, front, back, left, and right. Put on a blindfold and ask your helpers to take turns clapping their hands. Without turning your head when one of the helpers claps his or her hands, point toward the helper that you think is making the sound. Your helpers can count the number of times that you correctly pointed to the person making the sounds. Repeat the activity, turning your head to locate the sound.

BOOK LIST

Moore, Peter D. *The Encyclopedia of Animal Ecology.* New York: Facts on File, 1989. Information about animals, including those in grasslands.

VanCleave, Janice. *Animals.* New York: Wiley, 1993. Experiments about animals, including adaptive behavior. Each chapter contains ideas that can be turned into award-winning science fair projects.

TROPICAL GRASSLANDS

Tropical grasslands develop in the tropics. The grasslands in this area do not experience seasons determined by temperature, instead they have wet and dry seasons. These grasslands are not pure grasslands (grasslands made up only of grasses). Instead they are savannas, which are grasslands with scattered individual trees. Savannas cover almost half the surface of Africa and large areas of Australia, South America, India, and Southeast Asia.

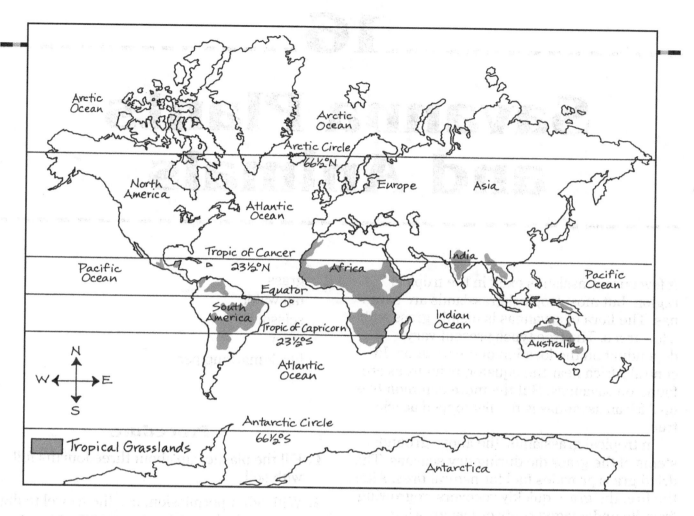

As with all biomes, climate is the most important factor in creating a savanna. Savannas are always found in warm or hot climates where the annual rainfall is from about 20 to 50 inches (50.8 to 127 cm) per year. This rain falls during six to eight months of the year, followed by a long period of drought when fires can occur. The fires and months of drought discourage the growth of trees and shrubs. Savannas that result from climatic conditions are called **climatic savannas.** But savannas are also created by other factors, such as soil conditions, and as the result of people clearing forest land for cultivation. When these fields are abandoned, grass takes over on the bare ground, and some trees can then grow here. Once developed, these man-made savannas are maintained due to climate and fires. In Africa, a heavy concentration of elephants in protected parkland have created a savanna by killing the trees so that grass takes over. The trees are killed when the elephants eat the trees' leaves and twigs and break off the branches, smashing the trunks and stripping the bark off trees. Elephants can convert a dense woodland into an open grassland in a short period of time. Again, climate and annual fires maintain the area as a savanna.

The animals that live in savannas have to adapt to great changes in the availability of food throughout the year; the wet season is a time of plenty, but during the dry season there are times of almost no food or water. Some of the savanna animals migrate to deal with this problem.

In this section, you'll investigate some of the plants and animals of savannas.

Savanna Plants and Animals

A few pure grasslands exist in the tropical region, but most tropical grasslands are savannas. The flora of savannas is mainly grass with a few trees. The tree types present vary, depending on the location of the savanna. In central Africa near the equator, palm trees are found on savannas. But the more common tree on African savannas is the flat-topped acacia tree.

In tropical grasslands, the above-ground stems of the grass die during dry seasons. This dried grass provides fuel for natural fires. After the fire, the grass quickly recovers, regrowing from its undamaged roots or fast-growing seeds. Since the fire moves so quickly across the savanna, the fire generally moves past a tree before it can catch on fire. So, trees may have some fire damage, but generally they are not severely injured.

FUN TIME!

Purpose

To determine why grass can survive being nibbled by savanna animals.

Materials

10-ounce (300-mL) plastic transparent cup
potting soil or soil from a garden
trowel

grass
tap water
scissors
ruler
black marking pen

Procedure

1. Fill the plastic cup about three-fourths full with soil.

2. With adult permission, use the trowel to dig up a small clump of grass.

3. Plant the grass in the cup of soil.

4. Moisten the soil with water. Keep the soil moist but not dripping wet during the experiment.

5. Use the ruler and scissors to measure and cut the grass stems so that they are about 1 inch (2.5 cm) above the soil.

6. Use the pen to color the ends of the grass blades.

7. Set the cup near a window that receives direct sunlight.

8. Measure the grass stems from their ends to the soil each day for 7 or more days. Make note of any growth above the colored ends of the grass.

Results

The grass grows, but there is no new growth above the colored ends.

Why?

Grass blades do not grow from the tips, as do other plants. Instead, they grow above each node along the stem. This type of growth allows grass to survive being nibbled by animals. When the tops of grass are eaten by animals or cut by a lawn mower, the grass continues to grow taller.

MORE FUN WITH SAVANNA ANIMALS!

While zebras may appear to look alike, each has its own individual stripe pattern, just as each person has his or her own fingerprint pattern. But there are similarities in the stripe pattern of each zebra species. The pattern on a zebra's hindquarters allow you to tell one kind of zebra from another, plus identify individual zebras. The hindquarters of two mountain zebras—Hartmann's Mountain and Cape Mountain—are shown. You can use your own fingerprint to model a distinctive pattern of zebra stripes. Rub the lead of a pencil back and forth across an index card. Then rub one fingertip back and forth over the pencil marking. Cover the smudged fingertip with a piece of transparent tape. Press the tape firmly against your fingertip. Carefully remove the tape and press the sticky side against a second white index card. Use the pencil to draw a frame around the fingerprint. Then add a tail, as shown.

BOOK LIST

Knope, Jim. *Natural Gardening.* New York: Time Life Books, 1995. A guide to show how to improve the ecology of where you live by learning about nature's animals and plants, including grasses.

VanCleave, Janice. *Ecology for Every Kid.* New York: Wiley, 1996. Fun, simple ecology experiments, including information about grass.

Hartmann's
Mountain Zebra
Equus zebra hartmannae

Cape
Mountain Zebra
Equus zebra zebra

Equus zebra _____
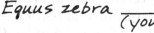
(your name)

Savanna Animal Survivors

There are differences and similarities among the animals in savannas in different locations. The similarities are generally with insects, such as ants and grasshoppers and with rodents, such as mice. In the African savannas, the animals include African elephants, giraffes, leopards, lions, zebras, aardvarks, ostriches, and red-billed oxpeckers. Australian savanna animals include dingos, kangaroos, wallabies, and wombats. South American savanna animals include deer, rheas, and capybara. Indian savanna animals include Asian elephants, Indian rhinocerous, tigers, and Indian gerbils. South East Asia savanna animals include Asian elephants, Asiatic Water buffalo, pygmy hogs, and tigers.

Animals in savannas have different adaptations for survival. Some migrate to deal with the lack of food during the dry season. There are herbivores that **graze** (feed on growing grass), such as zebras, and those that feed on leaves from shrubs and trees, such as giraffes. These animals have little protective covering in the open grasslands, but some are protected by **camouflage** (colors or patterns that conceal an object by making it blend with its background), such as mice, whose brown color blends in with the yellowish brown dried grass and shadows of its environment.

Many savanna animals have some protection from predators by being able to run fast, such as the giraffe and ostrich, which can both run at speeds of up to 35 miles (87.5 km) per hour. But the cheetah is faster than any other land animal. It can run short distances at 70 miles (112 km) per hour. Another advantage the cheetah has over other animals is that it can **accelerate** (to increase in speed) at an incredible rate. From standing still most adult cheetahs can reach a speed of 45 miles (72 km) per hour in two seconds, about the time it takes you to say "one thousand and one, one thousand and two." This is a faster acceleration than many race cars. Some animals, including rabbits and zebras, may be slower than their predators, but by zigzagging as they run instead of running in a straight path they have a chance of escaping.

Australian kangaroos can reach speeds of 40 miles (64 km) per hour, but only for a short time. It is their ability to leap more than 25 feet (40 km) while running at top speed that helps the kangaroo escape predators, such as dingoes. Kangaroos would rather flee than fight, but if necessary a kangaroo will hop into available water and stand chest deep. Then if a dingo swims out to attack, the kangaroo will grab the dingo and hold it next to its body with the dingo's head underwater until the dingo drowns. In shallow water, the kangaroo may use its back feet to hold the dingo under the water.

Some animals, such as the burrowing Indian gerbil, hunt at night when it is harder to be seen. Animals that burrow, including rodents, snakes, and some insects, are protected from predators by their underground home. Their burrows also protect these animals from grassland fires. By digging in the ground these animals help the grasslands by breaking up the soil so that air and water can more easily reach the roots of plants, mostly grass, growing there.

FUN TIME!

Purpose

To determine why patterns help camouflage animals.

Material

1 sheet of white copy paper
pencil
scissors
2 sheets of newspaper with mainly print on them
helper

Procedure

1. Fold the white paper in half twice.

2. Use the pencil to draw a rectangle about 2 by 4 inches (5 by 10 cm) on the folded paper.

3. Cut out the rectangle, cutting through all four layers of paper.

4. Repeat steps 1 through 3 using one of the newspaper sheets.

5. Place the remaining newspaper sheet on the floor.

6. Without anyone watching, place the eight rectangles on the newspaper.

7. Ask your helper to stand next to, but with his or her back to, the newspaper.

8. Tell your helper to turn and glance at the newspaper for 1 second and count the number of rectangular pieces you have placed on it. Time the glance by having your helper say "One thousand one," which takes about 1 second.

Results

Generally, the helper only counts the four white rectangles.

Why?

The rectangular pieces of newsprint were not only the same color of the newspaper but also had a similar pattern (the print) as the newspaper. The newspaper pieces were more camouflaged than the white pieces, so your helper probably only noticed the white pieces. In a similar way, the colors and patterns of many grassland animals help keep them hidden from predators and prey. The cheetah's light brown fur and black spots help camouflage it in the tall dried grass of the African savannas, enabling it to sneak up on its prey.

MORE FUN WITH SAVANNA ANIMALS

Impalas are antelopes found in African savannas. They can jump up about 10 feet (3 m) into the air, and while running, they can leap about 30 feet (9 m) forward in a single bound. This ability to jump and leap helps impalas escape predators. Other grassland animals, such as rabbits and grasshoppers, are also good jumpers. Make an animal hopper by cutting two 1-by-11-inch (1.25-by-27.5-cm) strips from stiff paper, such as a file folder. Lay the strips so that they form a right angle, as shown, and tape the ends together. Fold the bottom strip over the top strip. Now the top strip becomes the bottom strip. Repeat, folding the bottom strip over the top strip, until the strips are completely folded. Tape the ends together. This paper spring will be your animal hopper. Stand the animal hopper on a flat surface, such as the floor. Push the folds of the animal hopper together with one finger, then quickly slide your finger off one side and watch the animal hopper jump up. Invite a friend to make an animal hopper and have a jumping contest.

BOOK LIST

Legg, Gerald. *The World of Animal Life.* New York: Barnes & Noble, 1998. Facts about how impalas and other animals move, eat, hunt, defend themselves, and much more.

Walters, Martin, and Jinny Johnson. *Animals of the World.* Bath, UK: Dempsey Parr, 1999. A description of the anatomy, behavior, and habitats of over 1,000 animals.

VanCleave, Janice. *Ecology for Every Kid.* New York: Wiley, 1996. Fun, simple ecology experiments, including information and activities about grassland animals.

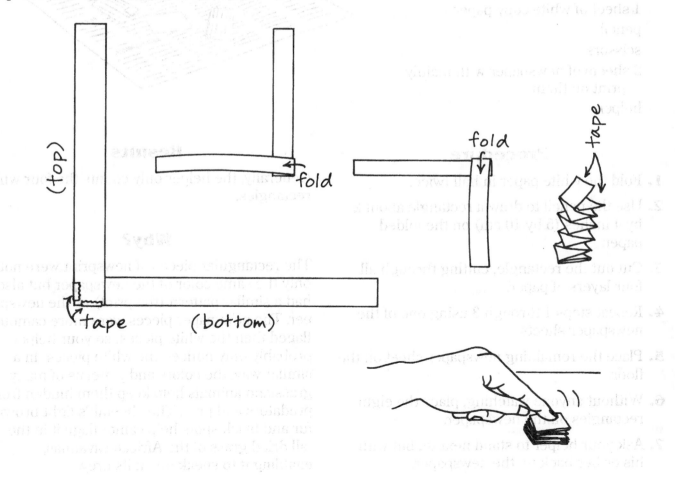

III

DESERTS

HOT DESERTS

COLD DESERTS

Deserts make up about 20 percent of Earth's land area, and most are located in the temperate zones. A desert is a biome that most people think of as hot and arid (dry). Actually, all deserts are arid, but temperaturewise, they can be either hot or cold. Whether a region is considered a desert is determined by the amount of rainfall and evaporation it receives. To be called a desert, a region has to have an average annual rainfall of less than 10 inches (25 cm) per year and an **annual evaporation rate** (measure of how much moisture evaporates from Earth's surface each year) that is greater than its precipitation (water that falls from the atmosphere in the form of rain, hail, snow, or sleet).

Daytime temperatures in **hot deserts** are generally very hot and can be as high as 131°F (55°C). **Cold deserts** have daytime temperatures that are below freezing for at least part of the year, and much or all of their precipitation comes from snow.

Both hot and cold deserts form as the result of several conditions, including how near they are to high mountain ranges, their distance from oceans, and high atmospheric pressure. **Atmospheric pressure** is the force that air in the atmosphere (blanket of gas surrounding Earth) exerts on a particular area. Most deserts form because of a combination of conditions, but there are four basic kinds of deserts, rain-shadow deserts, inland deserts, high-pressure deserts, and fog deserts.

A **rain-shadow desert** forms on the side of a mountain away from an ocean. The mountain acts as a barrier to rain. Moist air from the ocean rises quickly and cools. The moisture in the cooled air condenses and falls as rain. By the time the air passes over to the far side of the mountain it has lost most of its moisture. A desert forms on the far side of the mountain if the area does not receive moisture from another source. Hot rain-shadow deserts include the Mojave and the Sonoran in southwestern United States. Cold rain-shadow deserts include the Atacama in South America, the Great Basin in the United States, and the Takla Makan in China.

An **inland desert,** like a rain-shadow desert, forms because the air that sweeps over the area is dry and there isn't another source of moisture. In the case of an inland desert. Instead, because the region is a long way inland from an ocean, the moist air from the ocean loses most of its moisture before reaching the region. Two cold deserts, the Gobi in Mongolia and Takla Makan, can be classified as inland deserts. Simpson, a hot Australian desert, is also an inland desert.

An **air current** is the motion of air in a vertical, or nearly vertical, direction. Major air currents move over Earth in patterns that are affected by the temperature of the land. In some areas, such as the tropics near the equator, warm, humid air rises, forming clouds and rain. The rising air creates a zone of low atmospheric pressure. Low-pressure areas are associated with clouds and rain, so deserts are usually not found in these regions. After the warm air rises at the equator and loses most of its water, it circulates and descends near the Tropic of Cancer and the Tropic of Capricorn. The descending air produces high atmospheric pressure, which causes cloudless skies. This warm, dry, descending air evaporates (changes from a liquid to a gas) any moisture in the air above the ground, keeping the moisture from collecting and falling as rain. Thus the air doesn't bring in any rain, and it also prevents any rain clouds from forming. These conditions create a **high-pressure desert** (desert formed as a result of high atmospheric pressure). Hot deserts are commonly found in high-pressure areas of Earth, such as the Sahara and Kalahari deserts in Africa. But some cold deserts are high-pressure deserts, such as the Atacama on the coasts of Chile and Peru in South America, the Namib along the southwestern coast of Africa, and the Iranian Desert in Iran, Afganistan, and Pakistan.

Some high-pressure deserts are **fog deserts** because they are usually covered with fog (a cloud of water vapor just above Earth's surface). These deserts form along coasts with cold ocean currents. Cold wind moving over cold water carries very little moisture, but when this wind meets hot winds from the land, fog is formed. Two of the driest places on Earth, the Namib desert and the Atacama desert, are fog deserts.

Hot Deserts

Hot deserts are located in the temperate and tropical zones. Hot deserts have seasons that are generally warm throughout the year and very hot in the summer. It is not unusual on a summer day for the air to reach a temperature of 110°F (43°C). The desert floor may get as hot as 175°F (79°C) because of the lack of plants to provide shade. The hottest recorded

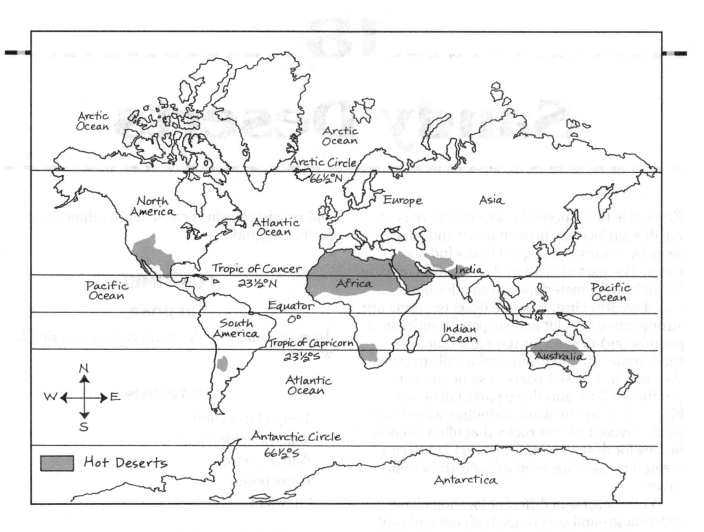

air temperature was 136°F (57.8°C) in El Azizia, Libya, located in the Sahara. The second hottest recorded air temperature was 134°F (56.6°C) in Death Valley, California, located in the Mojave Desert.

The difference between day and night temperatures in hot deserts can be great. This is due to the lack of cloud cover, which reflects sunlight, as well as a lack of moisture in the soil, which helps to hold in heat. Desert surfaces receive a little more than twice the solar energy received by humid cloudy regions and lose almost twice as much heat at night. Nighttime temperatures can be as much as 80°F (26°C) lower than daytime temperatures.

Most deserts, hot or cold, don't have very many plants. Most of the plants grow low to the ground, and all have special adaptations to survive the heat and lack of moisture, such as waxlike coatings on their surfaces, to prevent moisture loss. Plants that are adapted to growing in dry conditions are called **xerophytes.** The animals living in hot deserts also have special adaptations for survival. For example, some burrow underground and come out at night to hunt for food when it is cooler.

In this section, you will investigate the erosion of desert lands, plant transpiration, and some of the adaptations of plants and animals in hot deserts.

Sandy Deserts

Erosion is the process by which materials of Earth's surface are broken down and carried away by natural agents, such as wind and water. The part of erosion that involves only the breakdown of materials into smaller parts is called **weathering.** In some deserts, winds are strong enough to lift and suspend hundreds of pounds (kg) of sand for days at a time. The sand grains hit and grind against all surfaces they touch. The soft parts of structures are weathered first, and these parts fall or are blown away by the wind. Grinding, sand-filled winds create holes in rocks that often become homes for desert animals. Desert landforms created by blowing wind include arches and caves.

While deserts in different locations have different ground coverings, both hot and cold deserts have ground coverings that include sand, coarse or sandy soil, and pebbles. Erosion occurs in both hot and cold deserts. Where sand is present and winds are strong and blow from the same direction, hills of loose sand called **sand dunes** are formed. Areas with many sand dunes are called **dune fields,** which exist in hot deserts such as the Kalahari in southwestern Africa, the Arabian desert in the Arabian Peninsula, the Sahara in northern Africa, and cold deserts such as the Atacama along the coasts of Peru and Chile and the Takla Makan in western China. Sand dunes can change size as well as migrate (move to another location). Dunes on the hot Sahara desert can be over 800 feet (240 m) high. Some dunes migrate as much as 100 feet (30 m) per year, depending on the speed and duration of the wind. Faster winds

and consistent winds cause higher dunes and farther migrations.

FUN TIME!

Purpose

To determine why dry sand is easily carried by wind.

Materials

1 cup of dry sand
shallow baking pan
drinking straw
spray bottle
tap water

Procedure

1. Pour the sand into the pan.

2. Shake the pan so that the sand is as smooth and even in the pan as possible.

3. Hold one end of the straw at an angle to, and about 2 inches (5 cm) above, the surface of the sand.

4. Gently blow through the straw. You want to direct your exhaled breath toward the sand. *Caution: Remove the straw from your mouth before inhaling.*

5. Fill the spray bottle with water. Then wet the surface of the sand by spraying it with water.

6. Repeat step 4.

Results

The dry sand moves, forming small mounds, but the wet sand does not move.

Why?

Wet sand is heavier than dry sand. The lighter, dry sand grains are more easily picked up and carried by wind, forming sand dunes when dropped. In addition to the extra weight, wet sand sticks together, so it's harder for the wind to move it.

MORE FUN WITH SAND!

Some ancient sand dunes that were buried under more sand have changed into sandstone. **Sandstone** is a type of rock made from a buildup of layers of sand. Over time, as more sand is deposited, the layers are **compressed** (pushed together) and cemented, forming sandstone. Sandstone comes in a variety of colors, depending on the materials the sand is made of. The painted desert in Arizona is made of different colors of sand that have over time formed mountains of sandstone. You can make a model of layers of colored sand forming sandstone by putting layers of colored salt in a small jar. First, make four colors of salt. Measure 4 tablespoons (45 ml) of salt into four small bowls. Add 10 drops of one color of food coloring to one bowl of salt. Repeat with three more colors. Stir the salt every hour, or as often as possible until it dries. Spoon some of the salt into a small jar. Then add a layer of another color. Keep adding layers of colored salt until the jar is full. You can add designs to the colored layer by opening a paper clip and pushing its end into the salt right alongside the glass. Do not stir! Add more salt if needed to fill the jar, then put the lid on tight. Keep the jar upright and do not shake.

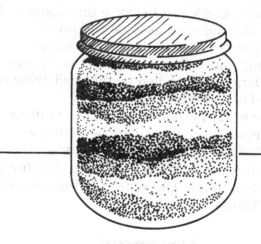

BOOK LIST

Bernard, Robin. *Deserts.* New York: Scholastic Professional Books, 1995. Information and hands-on activities about desert plants and other organisms and topics.

NatureScope: *Discovering Deserts.* Washington, D.C.: National Wildlife Federation, 1989. Information and activities about deserts.

VanCleave, Janice. *Earth Science for Every Kid.* New York: Wiley, 1991. Fun, simple earth science experiments, including information about erosion and sand dunes.

Transpiration

Plants give off water from their surfaces in a process called transpiration. This water leaves through stomata, which are tiny openings on the surface of a plant and are especially abundant on the undersides of leaves. Stomata open and close to let gases in and out. Water vapor is one of the released gases. Some leaves have more than a million stomata. In forests, trees need a large amount of water because about 98 percent of the water they take in is lost through the stomata. The leaves of tropical and temperate plants have stomata that are open longer periods of time and have larger openings than those of desert plants. In the desert, plants can survive with less water because the stomata of the plants do not open as wide and remain closed most of the time. The time stomata remain open as well as the size of their openings are largely controlled by the availability of water and of sunlight.

As the water evaporates from leaves during transpiration, more water is pulled into the plant at the roots. The water moves from the roots to the leaves through tubelike structures called xylem tubes. The water carries nutrients through plants.

FUN TIME!

Purpose

To determine how the number of stoma affects water loss.

Materials

4-by-8-inch (10-by-20-cm) piece of poster board

two 10-ounce (25-cm-diameter) plastic cups

pencil

scissors

paper hole punch

tap water

black marking pen

transparent tape

Procedure

1. Fold the poster board piece in half by placing the short sides together.

2. Stand one of the plastic cups upside down on the poster board.

3. Use the pencil to trace around the mouth of the cup on the poster board.

4. Cut out the circle tracing, cutting through both layers of the poster board.

5. Use the paper hole punch to cut 2 holes in one of the paper circles, one hole across from the other.

6. Randomly cut 20 holes in the other paper circle.

7. Fill the cups with an equal amount of water so that they are about three-fourths full with water.

8. Use the pen to mark a line on each cup that is even with the surface of the water.

9. Use the tape to secure the edges of one paper circle over the opening of each cup. You want the holes in the circle to be the only openings.

10. Set the cups near a window that gets direct sunlight.

11. After 3 or more days, compare the level of the water in each cup to the black water mark on each cup.

Results

There is less water in the cup with many holes in its cover than in the cup with only two holes in its cover.

Why?

The fact that the water level goes down shows that water has left the cups. Water in the cups evaporates, forming water vapor, which escapes through the holes in the covering. The amount of vapor escaping increases with the number of holes in the covering. The holes represent stomata in the leaves of plants. The more stomata in the leaves, the greater the amount of water lost by transpiration. Desert plants have fewer stomata, which are closed most of the time, as well as stomata with small openings, so they lose a smaller amount of water than do other plants, which have leaves containing many large stomata that are open most of the time.

MORE FUN WITH TRANSPIRATION!

The cactus is a plant found in many hot deserts. Cactus leaves are often modified not only to help the plant conserve water but also to protect the plant. For example, some cactus leaves have spikes to protect the plant, and some are hairy, making them less tasty to animals. Cactus leaves are generally very small or entirely absent, and some are covered with a waxy coating, which helps to hold water in the plant. A cactus without leaves, such as the barrel cactus or the saguaro, has stomata on its stem. Compare the amount of water added to the air by a cactus and a noncactus houseplant of equal size. Do this by covering the cactus and the leaves of a small houseplant with a large plastic bag. To make sure that only the water from the plants is collected and that the water does not leak from the bags, turn the plants on their sides and use a string to secure the bag around the base of the plants. Place a book on either side of the containers of the plants to keep the containers from moving. Allow the bags to remain over the plants for 24 or more hours. Then observe the amounts of water inside each. *Caution: Wear protective gloves when working with a cactus.*

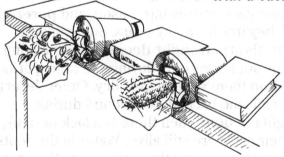

BOOK LIST

Bernard, Robin. *Deserts.* New York: Scholastic, 1995. Information and hands-on activities about the desert, including some on transpiration.

The Visual Dictionary of Plants. New York: Dorling Kindersley, Inc., 1992. A dictionary with photographs and descriptions of plant terms, including transpiration.

VanCleave, Janice. *Plants.* New York: Wiley, 1997. Experiments about plants, including some about transpiration. Each chapter contains ideas that can be turned into award-winning science fair projects.

Hot Desert Plants

Hot desert plants have adaptations that allow them to live in their hot, dry environment. Some desert plants have extremely long roots that can reach water 50 feet (15 m) or more below ground. Other desert plants have a network of roots that spread out just below the surface of the ground. These roots are able to quickly absorb water from dew or an occasional shower.

Desert plants have other adaptations, such as tiny leaves or no leaves at all. This prevents a lot of water from being lost through transpiration. (See chapter 19.) Desert plants with few or no leaves have green stems, and most or all of their photosynthesis occurs in their stems.

Plants, regardless of the biome where they are found, are called **annuals** if they live for only one year or growing season, and **perennials** if they live for many years. Some desert perennials are **drought-deciduous,** meaning they sprout leaves only during the rainy period, then drop them when it gets dry. Other desert perennials die back above ground during droughts (a time when there is a lack of rain), but their roots are still alive. Water in the roots of these plants keeps them alive until the next rain, when the plant will quickly send up shoots above ground. Desert perennials are among the oldest plants in the world, with some living many thousands of years. This age refers to the age of the root from which stems grow when there is enough moisture.

In hot deserts, a heavy rain generally occurs yearly, but in cold deserts, it rarely rains. For example, several hundred years may pass before it rains in the cold Atacama desert. After a hard rain, many deserts will suddenly be in bloom. This is because the seeds of many annual desert plants **germinate** (begin to grow) after a hard rain. Within only a few days, the plant has fully grown and a flower with seeds has been produced. But most of these fast-growing plants don't last long, and some don't even grow each year. Instead the seeds remain dormant (alive but inactive) until the necessary amount of rain has fallen. Scientists have found dormant seeds hundreds of years old that were still able to germinate. Since *annual* implies yearly, desert annuals are more accurately called **ephemerals,** which means they are short-lived. If their seeds were to sprout without enough water available to keep them growing, they would die. This doesn't generally happen because the seeds are covered with a protective coating that is washed off only by a hard rain. Once the chemical protective coating is washed off, the seed sprouts.

Some hot desert plants, such as the saguaro cactus, found only in the Sonoran desert, have a pleated or folded surface, much like an accordion. During wet periods, this folded surface expands, allowing the plants to hold a great deal of water. Plants in any biome that have thick and fleshy stems or leaves designed to retain water and reduce evaporation are called **succulents.**

FUN TIME!

Purpose

To determine how surface area affects evaporation rate.

Materials

2 paper towels
tap water
cookie baking sheet

Procedure

1. Wet the paper towels with water, then squeeze as much water out of each one as possible.

2. Lay one of the paper towels flat on the cookie baking sheet.

3. Fold the second sheet in half, then roll it up. Place it next to the flat paper towel on the sheet.

4. Position the sheet where it will receive direct sunlight.

5. When the open, flat towel is dry, which may take about 1 hour, unroll the other towel. How dry is that towel?

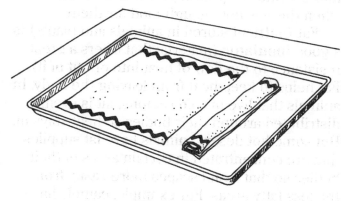

Results

The open flat paper towel dries out quickly, but after the same amount of time, the unexposed parts of the rolled towel are still moist.

Why?

The more surface area exposed to the air, the faster the water evaporates. Many desert plants are thick and round to help prevent water loss, such as the barrel cactus and saguaro in the hot Sonoran desert in the southwestern United States. Like the rolled paper towel, the small surface area of all desert plants helps keep water from evaporating quickly.

MORE FUN WITH EVAPORATION!

Not only does the smaller surface area of desert plants help reduce water loss, but some also have a waxy outer coating that helps keep water in. Try this activity to show how wax keeps water in. Tear a piece of bread in half. Lay one of the bread halves on a plate. Tightly wrap the second bread half in wax paper. Lay the wrapped piece of bread beside the unwrapped bread piece. Allow the bread to remain undisturbed overnight, then compare the softness of the unwrapped and wrapped pieces of bread. The firmer the bread the more water it has lost.

BOOK LIST

VanCleave, Janice. *Ecology for Every Kid.* New York: Wiley, 1996. Fun, simple ecology experiments, including information about desert plants.

Wallace, Marianne D. *America's Deserts: Guide to Plants and Animals.* Golden, Colorado: Fulcrum Publishing, 1996. Information about the plants and animals of North American hot deserts: Sonoran, Mojave, and Chihuahuan, and its cold desert Great Basin, as well as two unique regions within those areas, Death Valley and the Colorado Desert.

Hot Desert Animals

The kinds of animals in hot deserts vary greatly, depending on the physical features and plants of the area. Generally there are few or no large mammals living in deserts because they are not able to store water in their bodies and the desert provides little shelter from the hot sun. Most desert animals are **nocturnal animals,** which means they are active at night. Most stay deep underground in burrows where the sand is much cooler. Burrowing desert animals include the kangaroo rat, the badger, and the gopher. At night, after the sun goes down and the sand cools off, the animals come out to hunt for food. There are a few animals that are active during the day, such as beetles, hawks, and some lizards. But even these animals usually spend most of the day in whatever shade they can find.

The desert tortoise is found in the hot Mojave and Sonoran Deserts. This animal's front legs are muscular and flattened with long claws for digging. Its shell is from 9 to 15 inches (22.5 to 37.5 cm) long and about 4 to 6 inches (10 to 15 cm) high. It weighs about 8 to 15 pounds (3.6 to 6.8 kg). The desert tortoise spends about 95 percent of its life in underground burrows. Some burrows are as deep as 3 feet (0.9 m).

Because there is a lack of other water sources in a desert, some animals get all the water they need from the food they eat. For example, pack rats in hot deserts get water from the juicy plants they eat, such as the cactus. Snakes that eat pack rats, get water from the rat.

The kangaroo rat is another hot desert animal that gets water from the food it eats. This animal can live entirely on dry seeds without ever drinking water. These rats **rehydrate** (restore moisture) the dry seeds by storing the seeds in their burrows. The air in the burrows is humid, partly from moisture in the rat's exhaled breath. The dry seeds soak up some of the moisture from the air, so the rat gets some of the water from its own body back by eating the moist seeds.

Some animals sleep through especially hot, dry summer periods. This is similar to hibernation and is called **estivation** (dormant condition of some animals during the summer). Instead of sleeping through the winter, animals that estivate sleep through the hot summer when there is not enough food for them.

Fat (nutrient stored in animals and plants) is a good **insulator** (material that offers a great resistance to the flow of heat into or out of it). Fat helps to keep heat from leaving the body. In animals that live in cold regions, fat is evenly distributed around their bodies so heat stays in. But some hot desert animals have fat supplies that are concentrated in certain areas of their bodies so that heat escapes more easily from the less fatty areas. For example, camels have most of their fat in their humps, and the fat-tailed gecko has most of its fat in its tail.

Other body parts, such as large ears, can also help to keep an animals cool. The large ears of some animals, such as jackrabbits and foxes, do more than pick up sound. Air blowing over the large surface area of the ears helps to cool the blood in the ears, thus cooling the animal.

FUN TIME!

Purpose

To determine how having large ears helps hot desert animals cool off.

Materials

2 washcloths
index card

Procedure

1. Lay your arm on a table with the palm of your hand facing up.
2. Fold the washcloths in half twice. Place the two washcloths over your arm, leaving a very small crack between them.
3. Use the index card to fan the area of your exposed skin between the washcloths. Notice how cool the skin on your arm feels.
4. Separate the washcloths so there are about 3 inches (7.5 cm) of exposed skin between them.
5. Repeat step 3.

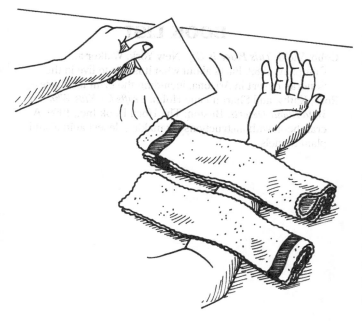

Results

Your arm feels cooler when there is a larger space between the washcloths.

Why?

Fanning the index card does not lower the temperature of the air, but it does move the air away from your skin. The layer of air next to your skin absorbs heat from your body. When you fan the air, this warmed air next to your skin is moved away, and cooler air takes its place. More heat is lost from your skin as it heats this air. Continued fanning continues this cycle of heat being lost from your skin. A similar cooling cycle occurs when a breeze blows on the oversized ears of some desert animals. Blood vessels in the ears are just under the skin. When air blows across this animal's ears, heat is transferred from the blood in the ears to the air above the ears, and the animal's blood is cooled. The cooled blood circulates through the animal's body as warmer blood moves to the ears and is cooled. In this experiment, the greater the surface area of skin that you fanned, the cooler your arm felt. The same is true for desert animals—the larger their ears, the more heat they lose and the cooler they become. This is also why animals that live in cold environments generally have tiny ears, so they do not lose so much heat.

MORE FUN WITH STAYING COOL!

Although many desert animals, such as the elf owl, kit fox, pack rat, and scorpion are nocturnal animals (feed at night), some are diurnal animals (feed during the day), such as the ground squirrel. Ground squirrels feed in the early morning and late afternoon, but they return frequently to their burrows to cool off and remain underground during the hottest part of the day. Ground squirrels also use their long bushy tails to provide shade. To provide shade a squirrel will flip its tail above its head and use it much like an umbrella or a hat. Make your own hat to keep you cool on a sunny day by following these steps:

- Fold a 20-by-20-inch (50-by-50-cm) square of colored paper, such as colorful wrapping paper, in half. Fold the paper in half again but in the opposite direction.

- Use a pencil to draw a curve on the folded paper, as shown. Cut along the curve, cutting through all four layers of paper.

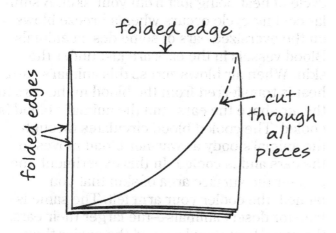

- Unfold the paper and cut along one of the folded lines to the center of the circle.

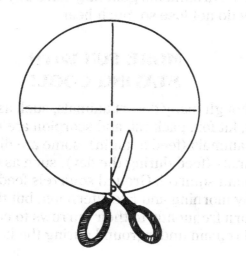

- Overlap and tape the edges of the circle to form a cone hat.

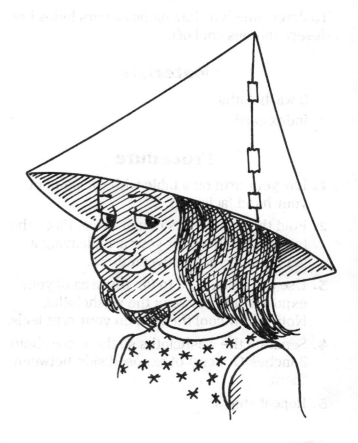

BOOK LIST

Cobb, Vicki. *This Place Is Dry.* New York: Walker and Company, 1989. Facts about what it is like to live in the Sonoran desert in Arizona, including the plant life there.

Ross, Kathy, and Sharon Lane Holm. *Crafts for Kids Who Are Wild About Deserts.* Boston: The Horn Book Inc., 1999. A craft book with instructions for making desert animal and plant models.

22

Camels

Camels are native to the deserts of Asia and North Africa. Two kinds of desert camels are dromedaries and Bactrians. Dromedaries have one hump and are best adapted for hot deserts. Bactrian camels, which have two humps, have adaptations for living in a cold desert. Most camels are **domesticated,** meaning they have been tamed so they can be used by humans. But a few Bactrian camels live in the wild in the remote grasslands of Mongolia, and some dromedaries that were taken to Australia now live wild in the outback. Domestic dromedaries are found mainly in the hot deserts of North Africa and Asia. Bactrian camels are mainly found in the cold, rocky Gobi desert in Asia.

Camels are the only animals that can carry heavy loads from place to place in the desert because they can go for long periods without eating or drinking water. A camel's hump doesn't carry water, as some believe. Instead the hump is filled with fat, which is a built-in food supply. This fat provides energy and water for the animal when food and water are scarce. When the fat is used up, the hump slumps over, but with rest and food the hump fills with fat and stands upright again.

Camels can go for weeks without a drink because they get some moisture from the food they eat and have stored as fat, and because their bodies have ways to prevent water loss. One physical adaptation a camel has for keeping water inside its body is a cavity in the camel's head. Dry air that the camel breathes in mixes with moisture in the cavity before moving through the camel's body, and moisture from the camel's breath is left in the cavity

when the camel exhales. When thirsty camels do drink, they can gulp down large amounts. Some drink as much as 35 gallons (140 liters) of water at a time. Camels like clean water and may even turn down dirty water. So camels often get the first clean water drawn from a well while the thirsty people wait until the camels are finished before they drink.

A short thick layer of fur protects camels from high daytime temperatures and prevents heat from escaping quickly when temperatures drop at night. Bactrian camels live in areas that get very cold in the winter, and their thick, shaggy, winter coats keep them warm. These heavy coats are shed during the hot summer months so the camels do not overheat.

Other physical adaptations that allow camels to survive in the desert include long eyelashes to protect their eyes from sunlight and blowing sand. Their eyes also have an extra thin eyelid that the camel can see through. Their extra eyelids can be closed during a sandstorm to protect their eyes. Camels can also shut their nostrils to keep sand out of their noses, and they also have large padded hoofs that help them walk on the sand.

A camel's behavior also helps it survive in the desert. On extremely hot days, a camel stays as cool as possible by resting. A camel will lie down in any available shady place or directly face the sun so that only a small part of its body receives the sun's rays. Because their body temperatures may be lower than the air temperature, a group of camels may lie down with their bodies pressed together. Camels usually walk slowly, at a speed of about 3 miles per hour

(5 km per hour), to keep from overheating. They walk by moving both legs on the same side together. This leg action produces a swaying, rocking motion much like that of a ship on water. Camels are sometimes called "ships of the desert."

FUN TIME!

Purpose

To determine how camels can walk across sand without sinking.

Materials

dime
lid from a 1-quart (1-liter) jar
4-by-4-inch (10-by-10-cm) square of corrugated cardboard
pencil
scissors
1 cup of sand or salt
cereal bowl

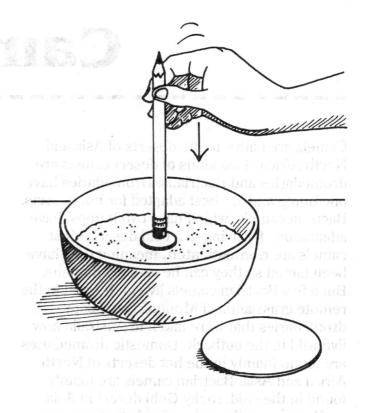

Procedure

1. Place the dime and lid on the cardboard. Use the pencil to draw an outline around each, then cut out the circles.

2. Pour the sand into the bowl.

3. Gently shake the bowl to make the surface of the sand smooth and level.

4. Place the small cardboard circle in the center of the sand's surface.

5. Stand the pencil on the cardboard circle, eraser end down.

6. Push down on the pencil and try to push the cardboard circle into the sand. Make note of how far the cardboard moves beneath the sand's surface.

7. Repeat steps 3 through 6, using the large cardboard circle.

Results

The small cardboard circle can be pushed beneath the surface of the sand but the large circle cannot be pushed under the surface.

Why?

Pressing against the larger cardboard circle results in the force being spread over a larger area. Like the large cardboard circle in this experiment, a camel's feet are large, so the weight on them is spread out. This allows camels to carry heavy loads and still walk easily on soft sand where trucks would get stuck. Some camels have feet as big as large plates.

MORE FUN WITH CAMELS!

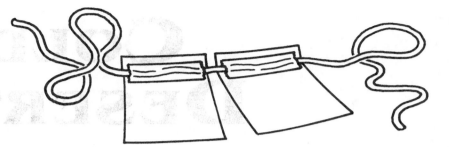

Camels have natural sun visors that help to shield their eyes from sunlight. These visors are made of bones that form broad ridges above their eyes. These bones stick out far enough to block sunlight when the Sun is overhead. Show how protrusions (something that sticks out) above your eyes can block sunlight. Make a paper visor for each eye by folding an index card in half, placing the small sides together. Unfold the card and cut across the fold. Lay the two card pieces side by side. Place a 36-inch (1-m) piece of string across the cards about ½ inch (1.25 cm) from one end of the cards. Tape the string to the cards. Bend the short end of the cards over the string. Tie the string around your head so that the short bent ends of the cards are against your forehead and above each eye. If necessary, bend the cards so that the long end of each card sticks out over your eyes. Stand under an overhead ceiling light or go outdoors when the Sun is overhead. Note how the papers block light from your eyes. *Caution: Never look directly at the Sun because doing so can permanently damage your eyes.*

BOOK LIST

Legg, Gerald, and Steve Weston. *The World of Animal Life*. New York: Barnes & Noble, 1998. Facts about how camels and other animals move, eat, hunt, defend themselves, and much more.

Mammals. Alexandria, Va.: Time-Life Books, 1997. Information about mammals, including camels.

Ruiz, Andres Llamas. *Animals on the Inside*. New York: Sterling Publishing Co., 1994. A book of discovery about the internal body parts of many animals, including the camel.

Walters, Martin, and Jinny Johnson. *Animals of the World*. Barth, U.K., 1999. Fact-filled and image-packed pages that investigate and describe the anatomy, behavior, and habitats of over 1,000 animals.

COLD DESERTS

Cold deserts have daytime temperatures that often are below freezing during part of the year. As in hot deserts, nighttime temperatures in cold deserts are much colder than daytime temperatures. The precipitation in cold deserts is either mainly or totally in the form of snow. The Gobi desert in Mongolia and the Great Basin Desert in North America are examples of

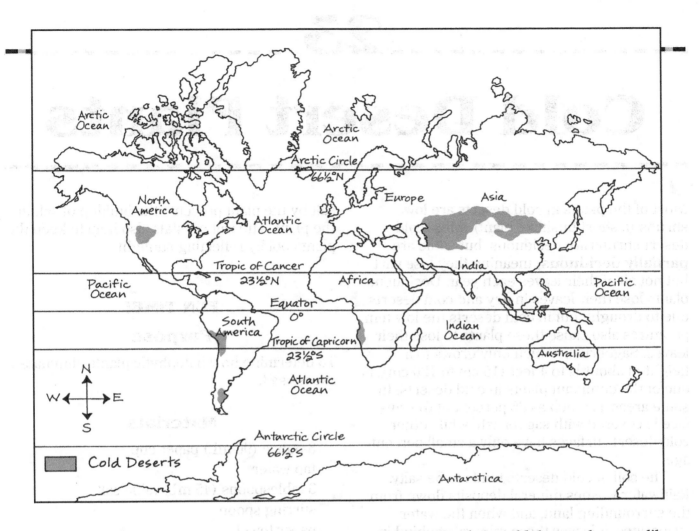

cold deserts. Some areas near the North and South Poles are as dry as a desert, but they are different from cold deserts in nonpolar regions because they are cold year-round, and have temperatures below freezing for all or most of the year. The deserts north of the Arctic Circle are called Arctic polar deserts, such as in northern Greenland. Deserts south of the Antarctic Circle are called Antarctic polar deserts, including the dry valleys in Antarctica's interior where it is reported that no rain has reached the ground in several million years. Precipitation evaporates before reaching the ground here.

Many animals in cold deserts burrow, like animals in hot deserts, but in the cold deserts it is to keep warm, not cool. That is why some of the same animals can be found in hot and cold deserts. Likewise, the same adaptations in plants are needed to survive in both types of deserts, so some of the same plants are found in both hot and cold deserts.

In this section, you will investigate the climate of a cold desert and the plants and animals found in cold deserts.

23

Cold Desert Plants

Most of the plants in cold deserts are low shrubs (a short bushlike plant). Most cold desert shrubs are deciduous, but some are **partially deciduous,** meaning they lose part but not all of their leaves each year. Deciduous plants lose their leaves in dry and cold deserts due to drought, but in cold deserts the low temperatures also cause these plants to lose their leaves. Sagebrush, which only grows to a height of about ½ to 4 feet (15 cm to 120 cm), is one of the dominant plants in cold deserts. In some areas as much as 85 percent of the surface is covered with sagebrush, while other cold desert surfaces have only a small percentage.

The soil of cold deserts tends to be salty. Rainwater washes mineral deposits down from the surrounding land, and when the water evaporates, it leaves these minerals behind in the soil. The world's largest salt flat is located in the Iranian desert, and the Bonneville Salt Flats and Great Salt Lake are located in the Great Basin desert. There are no plants growing in regions with very high salt concentrations. But surrounding these areas is generally a region of plants, including creosote bush and salt grass, then a narrow belt of shrubs, including greasewood and finally sagebrush.

Plants growing in salty soil of cold deserts have to be xerophytes (plants that are adapted to growing in dry conditions), **halophytic** (plants that are tolerant of salts in the soil), and have adaptations for the cold. The desert saltbush is such a plant. This shrub has tiny evergreen leaves that appear gray due to deposits of salt that are excreted (given off) by the plant onto the surface of the leaves. This release of

salt by the plant prevents the buildup of salt in the plant. The salt crystals also help to keep the plant cool by reflecting sunlight.

FUN TIME!

Purpose

To determine how halophytic plants eliminate excess salt.

Materials

3-ounce (90-mL) paper cup
tap water
3 tablespoons (45 mL) table salt
stirring spoon
paper towel
7-ounce (210-mL) paper cup
plate

Procedure

1. Fill the small cup about half full with water.

2. Add the salt to the small cup. Stir the water until as much of the salt as possible dissolves.

3. Fold the paper towel in half three times by placing the long sides together, then twist the folded strip. You have made a paper wick.

4. Set the cups on the plate as far apart as possible.

5. Hang one end of the dry, twisted paper towel strip in the cup of salty water. The end

of the paper towel needs to be at or near the bottom of the cup.

6. Hang the opposite end in the larger empty cup, forming a paper bridge between the cups.

7. Set the plate with the cups in a place where it will not be disturbed. Observe the paper towel wick and cup periodically for 7 or more days.

salty water

Results

The salty water moves through the paper wick, making it wet. In time, crystals of salt are seen on the paper wick.

Why?

The salty water moves through the paper wick in a way similar to how water moves from the roots through the xylem tubes of plants and out the stomata during transpiration. The water evaporates from the paper wick, leaving the salt on the surface of the paper much like the way

water evaporates at the surface of halophytic plants, leaving salt on the surface of their leaves.

MORE FUN WITH HALOPHYTIC PLANTS!

Salt grass is one of the few plants that can live in very salty soil without wilting. Salt grass takes the salt in, then sweats it out, leaving crystals on its blades for the rain to wash away. Grow epsom salt crystals on red construction paper. Cut a circle of red construction paper to fit in the bottom of a plate. Mix 2 tablespoons of Epsom salt with ¼ cup (63 mL) of water. Stir until as much of the Epsom salt as possible has dissolved. Pour the liquid mixture into the paper-covered plate. Make an effort not to pour out any of the undissolved crystals of Epsom salt. Set the plate in a place where it will not be disturbed until all the water evaporates. Observe the crystals of Epsom salt on the upper and lower surface of the red paper.

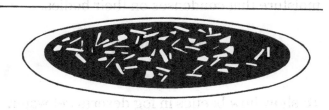

BOOK LIST

Bernard, Robin. *Deserts*. New York: Scholastic Professional Books, 1995. Information and hands-on activities about plants and other desert organisms.

NatureScope: Discovering Deserts. Washington, D.C.: National Wildlife Federation, 1989. Information and activities about desert topics.

Cold Desert Animals

While animals in dry deserts burrow underground to stay cool, burrowing animals in cold deserts do so to avoid the extreme cold. These burrowing animals include badgers, foxes, lizards, and many types of mice. Other animals found in cold deserts include bighorn sheep and jackrabbits. Deer are generally found only in the winter.

Two of the driest places on Earth—the Namib Desert on the southern coast of Africa and the Atacama Desert on the coasts of Chile and Peru—are cold, fog deserts. Darkling beetles in the Namib lie on their backs on top of sand dunes. Water from the fog condenses on the cool abdomens of the beetles and runs down into their mouths. Other animals in fog deserts, such as snakes and lizards, also drink moisture that condenses on their bodies.

FUN TIME!

Purpose

To show how beetles in fog deserts get water.

Materials

10-ounce (300-mL) transparent plastic cup
tap water
3 ice cubes

Procedure

1. Fill the cup half full with water.

2. Place the ice in the cup.

3. Place the cup in a humid area, such as the kitchen or the bathroom.

4. Allow the cup to sit for 5 to 10 minutes.

5. Observe the outside of the cup periodically for the presence of water. *Note: If the outside of the cup is dry, hold the cup near but not touching your mouth. Then breathe on the outside of the cup.*

Results

The outside of the cup looks cloudy, then tiny drops of water form on its surface. Some of the drops run down the side of the cup.

Why?

The icy water cools the surface of the cup. The air touching the outside of the cup cools, and the water vapor in the air condenses on the cool surface of the cup. At first the drops are so small they make the cup appear cloudy, but as more water collects, the water droplets combine forming drops large enough to see and some heavy enough to slide down the side of the cup. The removal of water from moist air in this experiment is similar to the way fog moving in from the coast condenses on the cool body of a cold fog desert beetle.

MORE FUN WITH ANIMALS!

To show how living in a burrow can keep animals warm in the winter, fill a 10-ounce (300 mL) plastic cup about one-fourth full with dirt. Stand a thermometer in the cup, then add more dirt so that the cup is about one-half full. With your fingers, gently press on the soil to pack it around the thermometer. Stand a second thermometer in an empty 10-ounce (300 mL)

cup. Allow both cups to sit undisturbed at room temperature for about 5 minutes. Note the temperature on both thermometers. Then sit the two cups in a freezer or outdoors if the temperature is near freezing. After 5 minutes, again read the temperature on the thermometers. Which has cooled more, the cup of soil or the cup of air?

BOOK LIST

Bernard, Robin. *Deserts*. New York: Scholastic Professional Books, 1995. Information and hands-on activities about plants and other desert organisms.

Bloom, Susan, and Maggie Ronzani. *Geography: Handy Homework Helper*. Lincolnwood, Ill.: Publications International, Ltd., 1998. A quick and easy reference guide about geography, including desert biomes.

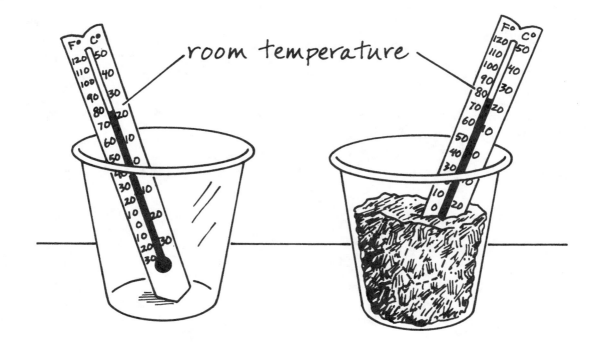

room temperature

IV

TUNDRA

LOWLAND TUNDRA

HIGHLAND TUNDRA

Tundra is a treeless biome that occurs in areas where the winters are long and cold and the summers are usually short and cool. The tundra is the simplest and least productive of all the biomes. The average yearly temperature of a tundra is below 32°F (0°C). Many tundras are called "cold deserts" because they receive such a small amount of precipitation. Some areas receive an annual precipitation of fewer than 5 inches (12.5 cm), which is less than many deserts, while other tundra areas receive over 80 inches (200 cm) per year. But overall, most tundras receive little precipitation.

One distinguishing characteristic of most tundra is its frozen ground. Even in the summer, the ground from one to five feet beneath the surface is frozen. This frozen ground is called **permafrost.** Most but not all tundra have permafrost, low precipitation, and constant winds.

Tundra are found in two different locations. One is at high latitudes, such as in the **Arctic** (region north of the Arctic Circle, and the **Antarctic** (region south of the Antarctic Circle). High-latitude tundra is also called **lowland tundra.** Most high-latitude (lowland) tundra is in the Arctic and is called the **Arctic tundra.** There is a small amount of tundra in the Antarctic, called the Antarctic tundra. The second location for tundra is at high elevations (on top of some mountains around Earth) and is called **highland tundra** or **alpine tundra.**

LOWLAND TUNDRA

The Arctic lowland tundras are known for being cold and dry with a short growing season of only about 50 to 60 days. The average winter temperature is –30°F (–34°C), and the average summer temperature is 37°F to 54°F (3° to 12°C). The warm but short summers

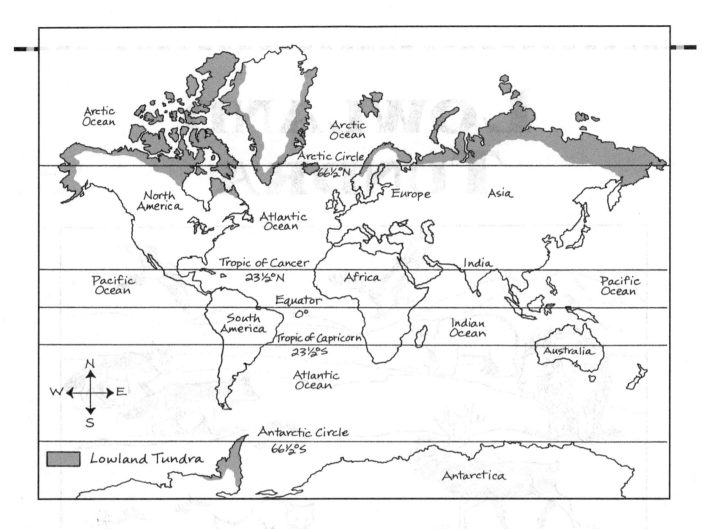

enable organisms to survive in this biome. Rainfall varies in different Arctic regions, with some regions receiving an annual precipitation of 40 inches (100 cm). But overall Arctic tundras are dry, with an average yearly precipitation of from 6 to 10 inches (15 to 25 cm), most or all of which is in the form of snow.

There is a small lowland tundra area above the Antarctic Circle on the peninsula of Antarctica. During the summer months, the plants found in the Antarctic tundra are mostly mosses, lichens, and algae. Most animals found here depend on the sea for food.

The winters in Arctic tundras are very cold, with 24 hours of darkness each day, and summers are warm, with 24 hours of light each day. The relative warmth of the milder seasons allows tundra organisms to grow and gather nutrients and energy to survive the cold season. Because the mild seasons are short, there are fewer kinds of organisms in the lowland tundras.

In this chapter, you will investigate permafrost, soil, and the plants and animals of Arctic tundras.

Permafrost

Permafrost is permanently frozen ground or ground in which a continuous temperature below 32°F (0°C) has existed for two or more years. Permafrost lies under about one-fourth of the world's land. Permafrost is more widespread and extends to greater soil depths in the Arctic tundras than in Alpine tundras.

Some tundra, such as lowland tundra in the far north, have continuous permafrost. Tundra farther south, such as in southwestern Alaska, have **discontinuous** (interrupted) or patchy permafrost, meaning there are areas with and some areas without permafrost. In these areas permafrost may not be present on south-facing slopes because the sloped ground faces the Sun and receives more direct sunlight, which warms the soil. Alpine tundras also generally have discontinuous permafrost. There is usually no permafrost beneath large deep lakes. Permafrost is also absent or rare on Alpine tundras at more southern locations, such as mountains in the tropics.

The surface layer of permafrost that thaws and refreezes each year is called the **active layer.** This layer is where plants can grow during the warm periods. Depending on the location, the active layer varies in depth from a few inches (cm) to several feet (m). The farther north you go, the more shallow the active layer is because the temperature is colder and less of the permafrost melts. Heat from buildings, roads, railways, and other structures may thaw massive amounts of ice in permafrost, often causing damage to the structures. Heat from buildings sitting too close to the ground can cause the permafrost to melt, and the building can sink into the ground. To prevent this from happening, buildings and other types of structures built on permafrost are generally raised above the ground on pillars.

Fossil remains that have been found in permafrost provide clues to the age of the permafrost formation. For example, mammoths have been found frozen in Arctic permafrost. These animals became extinct about 10,000 to 15,000 years ago, so the permafrost where the mammoths were found must be about that old.

During the short warm summer, the upper layer of the frozen land melts and the frozen layer beneath prevents the water from draining. This results in the Arctic tundra having water-saturated soils during the summer. The solid permafrost during the winter and soggy, water-soaked soil during the summer restrict the kind of plant life that can grow here. But there are about 1,700 different kinds of plants living in the tundra biomes, including mosses, lichens, grasses, and short shrubs. There are no trees. All the plants have shallow root systems because of the permafrost.

FUN TIME!

Purpose

To determine how permafrost affects the germination of seeds.

Materials

1 cup (500 mL) soil
cereal bowl
tap water

two 10-ounce (300-mL) plastic cups
spoon
12 dried beans (pinto or lima work well)
toothpick

Procedure

1. Pour the soil into the bowl.

2. Add enough water to the soil to moisten it. Stir the soil as the water is added.

3. Pour half of the moistened soil into each cup.

4. Use the spoon to dip out about 1 inch (2.5 cm) of moistened soil from one of the cups. Scatter 6 beans on the surface of the soil in the cup. Then cover the beans with the soil that was removed.

5. Repeat step 4, using the remaining cup and beans.

6. Place one cup in the freezer and the other on a table at room temperature.

7. Keep the cup of soil at room temperature moist but not wet. Add equal amounts of water to both cups.

8. After 24 hours, try to stick a toothpick in the soil in each cup.

9. Keep one cup in the freezer and the other at room temperature for 7 or more days. Observe the surface of the soil in each cup every day for evidence of plant growth.

Results

The toothpick easily enters the soil at room temperature but will not enter the frozen soil. Beans grew in the warm, soft soil but did not grow in the hard, frozen soil.

Why?

Permafrost is ground that is frozen for two or more years. The ground may contain rock, sand, or soil. In most permafrost, as in this experiment, ice surrounds the material in the ground creating a firm, solid mass that is difficult to penetrate. Seeds cannot germinate (begin to grow) in the ice for several reasons. First, seeds need water to grow, and the water molecules in the ice are bound together and unavailable to the seeds buried in the frozen

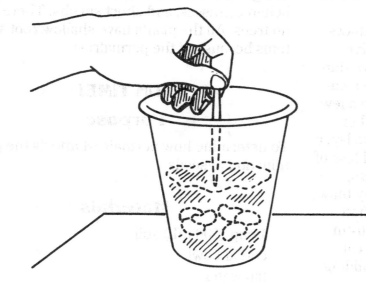
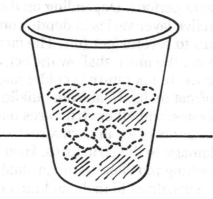

ground. Second, seeds generally need a temperature above freezing to grow. So most plants in the tundra are not grown from seed. Instead they grow from roots that live from year to year. Even these plants cannot grow in the hard, dry permafrost because their roots and stems cannot penetrate the ice. Plants can only grow in unfrozen soil above the permafrost, if there is any. The depth of plant roots depends on the depth of the unfrozen soil, which varies from a few inches to a few feet. Cold permafrost also cools any unfrozen soil above it. Cold soil slows root growth and reduces the ability of roots to take up water.

MORE FUN WITH PERMAFROST!

In the tundra, at a certain depth in the ground, there is an **inactive layer** of permafrost, which means it never thaws. The surface of an inactive layer is called the **permafrost table.** Water cannot penetrate the permafrost table. In low-lying areas pools of water can form on the permafrost. Even with low rainfall, the active layer can become very wet because the underlying permafrost keeps the moisture near the surface. Prepare a model of snow-covered permafrost with a thin active layer. Do this by ask-

ing an adult to prepare your favorite gelatin. Fill half a transparent bowl with the gelatin mix. Place the bowl in a refrigerator. When the gelatin gels, remove the bowl and cover the gelatin with a layer of crushed brown cookies, such as Oreos. Ask your adult helper to crush the cookies in a blender or place the cookies in a plastic bag and roll a rolling pin back and forth across the bag several times. Place vanilla ice cream on top of the cookie layer. The ice cream represents snow, the cookies are thawed permafrost (active layer), and the gelatin is the permafrost. Place the bowl on a table and observe what happens to the melted ice cream. Does it sink into the permafrost? If the materials and utensils have been kept clean, you can eat the contents of the bowl when you're through observing.

BOOK LIST

The Alaska Almanac. Anchorage, Alaska: Alaska Northwest Books, 1998. Facts about Alaska, including its permafrost.

Foreman, Michael H. *Arctic Tundra.* Chicago, Ill.: Children's Press, 1997. Informative book on the plants and animals of the Arctic tundra.

Silver, Donald M. *One Small Square: Arctic Tundra.* New York: Learning Triangle Press, 1994. Facts and fun activities about the Arctic tundra, including permafrost.

Arctic Tundra Plants

The growing season in the Arctic (lowland) tundra only ranges from fifty to sixty days per year because of the lack of light and heat. This growing season occurs during the summer, when temperatures average between 37°F and 54°F. All tundras, regardless of their location are characterized by grasses and grasslike plants (such as sedges), lichens, and dwarf forms of woody plants. Although there are about 1,700 kinds of plants in the Arctic tundras, there are no plants with deep root systems, such as trees. This is partially due to the low temperature and low precipitation, but mainly due to the layer of permanently frozen subsoil.

Conditions are most severe during the winter, but cool temperatures and strong winds during the summer also present problems to organisms in the tundra. Most of the plants are small and grow close to the ground. This helps them survive in the Arctic because the wind speed is slower near the ground due to friction between the wind and objects on the surface, including rocks and other plants. The air temperature near the ground is also warmer because the soil absorbs and radiates some heat from the Sun. To survive the cold winter, the above-ground growth of many plants dies, while their main growth and energy storage remains alive in their underground roots.

The coloration of organisms in the tundra is another adaptation to their cold environment. Since dark colors absorb sunlight and light colors reflect it, there are more dark plants than light plants in the tundra than in warmer environments. Many tundra plants are purple or blue. Light-colored flowers in the tundra are **heliotropic,** which means they turn to face the Sun to gather light and warmth.

FUN TIME!

Purpose

To determine how the shape of flower petals helps seed production of some Arctic plants.

Materials

2-by-2-inch (5-by-5-cm) square of aluminum foil
2-by-2-inch (5-by-5-inch) square of black construction paper
transparent tape
desk lamp

Procedure

1. Overlap the edge of the foil and the black paper square. Secure with tape.

2. Lay the combined strip on a table about 12 inches (30 cm) from a lamp, with the black paper facing the lamp.

3. Bend up about 1 inch (2.5 cm) of the black paper facing the lamp. The bent edge should cast a shadow across the remaining black paper.

4. Use the tape to secure the black paper to the table.

5. Lift the aluminum foil strip and slightly squeeze the edges so that the foil curves. Change the height of the foil and its curve

tape
black paper
foil

to form a spot of light in the center of the shaded black paper taped to the table.

Results

Lifting the foil causes light to hit the shaded black paper. Curving the foil causes a spot of light to form in the center of the paper.

Why?

The light coloration of Arctic poppies and other light-colored flowers in this tundra is an adaptation to the cold environment. The flowers of these plants are heliotropic, which means they turn to face the sun to gather more light and warmth. Turning toward the Sun helps to direct sunlight onto the darker, shaded center of the flower, where the seeds are produced, and the shape of the leaves helps to focus the Sun's light on the flower's center. Insects that live in the center of these flowers also benefit from the sunlight focused here.

MORE FUN WITH TUNDRA PLANTS!

Because permafrost prevents trees from growing long roots, it is a primary reason why trees do not grow in the tundra. Demonstrate that short plants can stand with short roots but tall plants cannot. Do this by laying an index card on a table. Divide a grape-size ball of clay into two parts, making one part pea-size. Shape each of the clay pieces into a ball. Spread the small clay ball in the center of the card. Make the clay layer about as big around as a dime. Stick the larger clay ball on the end of a piece of uncooked fettuccine. Stand the free end of the fettuccine in the center of the clay on the card, pushing the fettuccine as far as possible into the clay. Be careful not to break the fettuccine.

Release the fettuccine and observe any movement. *Note: The fettucine should fall. If not, use a longer piece of fettucine. If the fettucine falls, repeat the procedure, using shorter pieces of fettucine until it is short enough to remain standing in the clay.*

BOOK LIST

Foreman, Michael H. *Arctic Tundra.* Chicago, Ill.: Children's Press, 1997. Informative book on the Arctic, including the plants and animals that live there.

Silver, Donald M. *One Small Square: Arctic Tundra.* New York: Learning Triangle Press, 1994. Facts and fun activities about plants and animals of the Arctic tundra and the land they live on and in.

Arctic Tundra Animals

Much of the year, the Arctic (lowland) tundra is very cold. Tundra animals have physical and behavioral traits that help them survive and produce young in this harsh environment. Arctic tundra plants do not grow during the long winter months. So food is scarce. Animals living here must adapt their behavior in order to survive with limited or no food for long periods of time. Some animals avoid the long months of cold and lack of food by migrating to warmer environments with more food. Caribou migrate and spend the winter in southern forests. Many tundra fish even migrate to places where water remains liquid through the winter. Many tundra birds fly thousands of miles to areas in Central and South America. The Arctic tern migrates about 10,000 miles (16,000 km) to winter in Antarctica. This bird spends most of its life in daylight, living in the Arctic when it is daylight for several months, then flying to the Antarctic to stay for its daylight period.

Many tundra animals remain active during the winter by living under the snow and eating the buds, stems, and roots of dormant plants. Some, such as pikas and singing voles, also remain active under the snow layer and eat grasses and other plants they stored during the warm growing season.

Some animals survive by reducing their activities to a minimum. For example, the Arctic ground squirrel and marmots hibernate. A ground squirrel's normal body temperature of 97°F (36°C) drops to about 62°F (17°C) during hibernation. Its normal heart rate of 200 to 400 beats per minute drops to 7 to 10 beats per minute, and it breathes about 3 times per minute instead of its normal 60 times per minute. With a lower heart rate the squirrel needs only about 2 percent of its normal amount of energy. Hibernating animals store the needed energy as layers of fat, which are used by their bodies during the time they hibernate. During hibernation the squirrel doesn't eat or drink, instead its body uses the stored fat for energy.

Some animals, such as black and brown bears, reduce their activity during the cold winter by sleeping in a **den** (shelter for animals in nature) for several months. But these bears are not true hibernators. The difference is that the heart rate of a denning bear is reduced from about 50 to 60 beats per minute to about 20 beats, but its body temperature is not reduced. A brown bear weighing 300 pounds (136 kg) in the autumn may lose 100 pounds (45 kg) during its long winter nap. Bears wake up quickly if disturbed, but hibernating squirrels will not wake until their body temperature rises due to a change in the temperature of its environment.

FUN TIME!

Purpose

To determine your body mass index (BMI).

Materials

calculator

Procedure

1. Determine your weight in kilograms by dividing your weight to the nearest pound by 2.2.

   Example: If your weight is 88 pounds your weight in kilograms (kg) would be:

   $$88 \text{ pounds} \div 2.2 = 40 \text{ kg}$$

2. Determine your height in meters by dividing your height in inches by 39.4.

   Example: If your height is 53 inches your height in meters would be:

   $$53 \text{ inches} \div 39.4 = 1.35 \text{ m}$$

3. Find you height in square meters by multiplying your height in meters by itself.

   Example:

   $$1.35 \text{ m} \times 1.35 \text{ m} = 1.81 \text{ m}^2$$

4. Calculate your BMI by dividing your weight in kilograms (step 1) by the square of your height in square meters (step 3). Your BMI is the magnitude of this weight: height square ratio.

   Example:

   $$40 \text{ kg} \div 1.81 \text{ m}^2 = 22.09 \ \frac{\text{kg}}{\text{m}^2}$$

   $$\text{BMI} = 22.09$$

Results

The BMI calculated from the weight and height in the example is 22.09.

Why?

Like animals in any biome, your input energy comes from the food that you eat. Output energy is what you need for basal metabolism and activities. **Basal metabolism** is the amount of energy used by the body while resting or **fasting** (not eating) to carry out basic functions, such as breathing, making your heart pump, and growing. An animal with a high basal metabolism needs more input

energy than one with a lower basal metabolism. A more active animal also uses more energy. So animals with a higher basal metabolism and those that are more active need more food to provide the needed energy. Animals have a lower basal metabolism during the winter when they are hibernating than during the summer when they are not hibernating and are active.

Arctic animals that hibernate prepare for winter by eating more and storing up fat. Thus they increase their **body mass index (BMI),** which is the ratio of their body weight (in kilograms) to the square of their height (in meters). As they hibernate or sleep during the winter without eating, they lose weight, and by spring they have a lower than normal BMI. The average BMI for human boys is 22 to 24 and for girls is 21 to 23. With a BMI of 22.09, the example child (boy or girl) in this experiment falls in the average or 50th percentile. Although a high BMI indicates **obesity** (the condition of being overweight), there are exceptions. For example, an athletic person can have a high BMI because of an increase in muscle mass rather than mass due to fat. Muscle has a greater **density** (a measure of the mass of a given volume of material) which means that when equal volumes of fat and muscle are compared, muscle has a greater mass. So, check with your physician to see if your BMI is average.

MORE FUN WITH ANIMALS!

During the 6 to 7 months of winter, when an Arctic ground squirrel hibernates, its heartbeat slows. Count your own heart rate and note that while it does not drop as much as a hibernating squirrel, it is slower when you are inactive. Do this by laying your arm on a table with the palm

of your hand up. Place the fingertips of your other hand below the thumb on your upturned wrist. Gently press until you can feel your heartbeat. *Note: You may have to move your fingertip around the area until you feel your heartbeat.* Count the number of heartbeats in 15

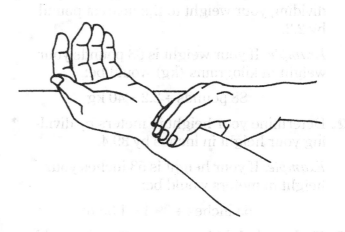

seconds. Then multiply the number by 4 to calculate your heartbeat per minute. Repeat this procedure after you have performed an energetic activity, such as jumping up and down or sitting and raising your hands up and down 10 or more times. Compare the results.

BOOK LIST

Green, Jen. *On the Tundra.* New York: Crabtree Publisher, 2002. Information about wolves, polar bears, as well as astonishing facts about small birds and insects that travel many miles to breed in the Arctic tundra.

Ranger Rick's NatureScope: Amazing Mammals Part I. Washington, D.C.: National Wildlife Federation, 1988. A general introduction to mammals, including how mammals adapt to cold environments.

Mammals. Alexandria, Va.: Time-Life Books, 1997. Information about mammals, including bears.

Parker, Steve. *Natural World.* New York: Dorling Kindersley, 1994. A view of the natural world at rest and on the move, including information about hibernation.

Polar Bears

Most of the Arctic Ocean's surface is frozen for most of the year, but it partially melts and breaks in the summer to form bands of relatively open water along some coastlines. When the ice in the southern part of the Arctic Ocean melts, most of the polar bears move north to stay on the ice, but some move south and spend the summer on the tundra. Most of these bears migrate to the same areas each summer and winter year after year in search of food. Ringed seals are their main source of food, but they occasionally also eat bearded seals, walruses, fish, mussels, and berries. Some have even found garbage dumps easy hunting. During the spring, when seals are easy to find, the bears eat so many seals that they get quite fat, some gaining more than 200 pounds. This fat is used up during the winter when the seals are more difficult to find.

Seals are very fast in the water, but polar bears are unusually clever at solving problems in order to obtain food. Since these bears have an extraordinary sense of smell, they can smell the seals even through thick layers of ice. Polar bears observe and learn that seals come out of holes in the ice. If they smell a seal beneath the ice, then they will commonly sit and wait by a hole in the ice for a seal to come out. A polar bear may patiently wait for hours by the hole. When the seal appears the bear, with lightning speed, slaps the seal with its giant paw and pulls the seal out through the hole.

When a bear spots a seal on the ice, it will try to sneak up on it. The bear is careful to stay downwind, which means the wind blows from the seal toward the bear so the seal does not smell the bear. The white color of the polar bear's fur allows the bear to be camouflaged in the snow and ice, so it can better stalk its prey. Since it is not easily seen when it lays flat on the ice on its belly, the bear can slowly creep toward a seal and grab the seal before it can escape into the water. To catch a seal lying near the water's edge, a bear will swim quietly toward the seal, then dive under the water so it can spring to the surface and lunge at the unsuspecting seal.

Polar bears are the only marine bears. They are expert swimmers and have been known to swim as far as 50 miles (80 km). In comparison to other bears, their bodies are longer and more **streamlined** (shape offering the least resistance to motion through fluids, which are gasses or liquids). Polar bears are large, strong, and very fierce. Their very broad front feet help them swim. They paddle with their front legs and steer with their rear legs. The thick layer of fat under the bear's skin called **blubber** helps it to stay warm in the icy Arctic water.

All polar bears look white, but each hair is actually a transparent tube. Some of the light hitting the transparent hair is scattered, in the same way that light hitting the water in clouds is scattered, causing the hair and clouds to look white. Some light hitting the hair passes through the tubes, where it is absorbed by the bear's skin, which warms the bear. The skin of polar bears is actually black, but the fur is so thick that it totally covers the black skin.

Polar bear fur is made up of long hairs separated by short hairs. The long hairs keep the skin dry and warm. The short hairs create spaces where air is trapped. Trapped air is a good insulator, so it helps to warm the bear. To warm up, the bear can fluff up his fur, which traps more air. To cool off, the bear can slick his fur down, which pushes out air. The fur becomes thicker in the winter, and some is shed in the spring in preparation for the warmer summer season.

Polar bears are the largest land predator. The largest polar bear ever measured was a male that stood more than 11 feet (3.3 m) tall when standing on its hind legs and weighed 2,210 pounds (1,005 kg). The average range for head and body length is 6 to 8 feet (1.8 to 2.4 m). Most male polar bears weigh an average of about 880 pounds (350 kg), and most females weigh about 550 pounds (250 kg). Almost everything about a polar bear is big, except its ears, which are tiny to prevent heat loss from the body.

FUN TIME!
Purpose

To demonstrate how the hair on a polar bear's feet helps prevent the bear from sliding on ice.

Materials

  2 unopened cans of tuna or other small cans
    of equal size
  washcloth
  rubber band
  shallow, metal baking pan, such as a cookie
    sheet

Procedure

1. Cover one of the cans with the washcloth. Bring the sides of the cloth together and secure them with the rubber band, as shown.

2. Place the covered and uncovered cans side by side on one end of the pan.

3. Slowly raise the end of the pan where the cans sit until both cans slide down the pan. Note which can moves first as well as which moves faster.

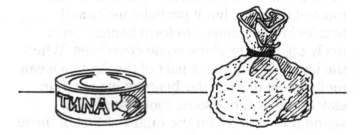

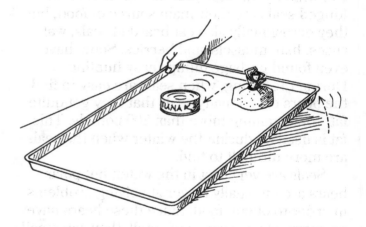

Results

The uncovered can moves first, and it moves faster than the covered can.

Why?

All bears have **plantigrade feet** (feet whose heel and sole touch the ground when an animal or human walks) and five claws. But unlike other bears, polar bears have hair on the bottoms of their feet, which protects their feet from the cold and helps keep the bear from sliding on the ice. Like the feet of a polar bear, the cloth-covered can doesn't slide very easily.

MORE FUN WITH POLAR BEARS!

Even though they are very large and heavy, polar bears are able to jump over cracks in ice more than 20 feet (6 m) wide. Compare how far you can jump with the distance that a polar bear can jump. Do this by cutting a string 20 feet (6 m) long. In a large open outside area, stretch out the string. Cut another string 2 feet (0.6 m) long and lay it at one end of the long string. The short string will be the starting line.

Back away from the starting line far enough to get a running start. Then run toward the string. When you reach the starting line, jump as far as you can. Ask your helper to mark where you land by standing next to the spot. Were you able to jump as far as a polar bear?

BOOK LIST

Burton, John. *Mammals of North America*. San Diego: Thunder Bay Press, 1995. Fun facts and activities about North American animals, including the polar bear.

Foreman, Michael H. *Arctic Tundra*. Chicago, Ill.: Children's Press, 1997. Informative text with emphasis on the plants and animals of the Arctic tundra.

Legg, Gerald, and Steve Weston. *The World of Animal Life*. New York: Barnes & Noble, 1998. Facts about how polar bears and other animals move, eat, hunt, defend themselves, and much more.

20 feet (6 m)

(start)

HIGHLAND TUNDRAS

The highland or alpine tundra are treeless mountain areas that are located high on mountains and extend from the timberline to the top of the mountain or to the ice cap region at the top. Much highland tundra consists of barren rock or a cover of thin soil. But there are areas with deep soil and abundant plant cover. The different types of plants grow in patches, and the types of plant growth depend on different factors, including

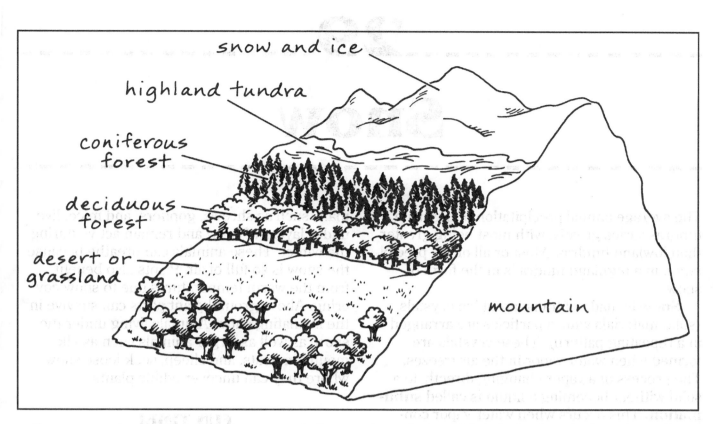

snow and ice

highland tundra

coniferous forest

deciduous forest

desert or grassland

mountain

soil, exposure to wind, and snow accumulation.

Highland tundras are found throughout the world, even at the equator on Mount Cayambe in Ecuador, which has an elevation of almost 19,000 feet (5,700 m). The highland tundra growing season is about 180 days, and nighttime temperatures are usually below freezing. Unlike the lowland tundra, most of the ground of highland tundra is on a slant, so highland tundra soil is generally well drained.

Cold weather occurs in highland tundras for different reasons than in the lowland tundras. Air at low elevations is more **dense** (having parts closely packed together) than at higher elevations. Air acts as an insulator (material that offers a great resistance to the flow of heat into or out of it), keeping some of the heat from Earth's surface from escaping. Thus the air in Earth's atmosphere acts like a blanket that keeps Earth's surface warm. But it also blocks some **solar energy** (energy from the Sun, including light and heat) from reaching Earth. Because the atmosphere is less dense on mountaintops, more solar energy reaches the ground. But the less compact air

is such a poor insulator that the heat is easily lost. Thus the atmosphere traps little heat, and nighttime air temperatures at high elevations are often 50°F (27°C) or more lower than those at midday at the same elevation. The average daily (day and night combined) air temperature drops about 3°F (1.6°C) for every 1,000 feet (300 m) increase in elevation. Thus, the temperature at the top of Mount Cayambe at an elevation of 19,000 feet (5,700 m) is about 57°F (31°C) cooler than at its base.

Many alpine tundras have seasonal patterns similar to Arctic tundras. However, as one moves closer to the equator, alpine tundras experience no seasonal changes in temperatures. Instead, warm and in some places even hot temperatures occur during the day, while bitterly cold temperatures occur at night. Thus instead of seasonal warm and cold seasons, periodic temperature changes occur each day.

In this chapter, you will investigate two physical features of alpine biomes, snow and wind, and how they affect the animals and plants of these regions.

Snow

The average annual precipitation of highland tundras varies greatly, with most being greater than lowland tundras. Most or all of the precipitation in a highland tundra is in the form of snow.

Snow is made of transparent ice crystals (solid materials whose particles are arranged in a repeating pattern). These crystals are formed when water vapor in the air freezes. The process of a vapor changing directly to a solid without becoming a liquid is called **sublimation.** This occurs when water vapor condenses at temperatures below the freezing point. As snow crystals fall and collect on the ground, air becomes trapped among the crystals. Thus snow is puffed up with air, making it not only soft and fluffy but also larger in volume than the water it is made from. So when 1 inch (2.5 cm) of snow melts it will not produce 1 inch (2.5 cm) of water. A measurement for annual precipitation is a measurement of liquid water. For example, if snow is the only precipitation, and the average annual precipitation is 20 inches (50 cm), this annual precipitation measurement means that enough snow falls to equal 20 inches (50 cm) of rain.

Air is a good insulator, so it helps to keep heat from escaping. Because of the trapped air in snow, snow is a good insulator. In the tundra, snow acts like an insulating blanket that traps some of the heat given up by the ground. Ground covered by air-filled snow cools slowly because of the insulating snow. Thus when the air temperature is below freezing, 32°F (0°C), the ground covered by snow is warmer than the air above the snow. Many small tundra animals, such as shrews, gophers, and mice, live under layers of snow and remain active during the winter. These animals can breathe because the snow is so full of air. Plants also benefit from the warm temperatures due to snow covering. Above-ground plant parts can survive in the insulating snow. Animals living under the snow, as well as larger animals such as elk, mountain goats, and sheep, seek loose snow where they can uncover edible plants.

FUN TIME!
Purpose
To measure the volume of melted snow.

Materials
masking tape
straight-sided transparent plastic drinking
    glass at least 5 inches (12.5 cm) tall
metric ruler
pen
snow (shaved or finely crushed ice will
    work if snow is not available)

Procedure
1. Place a strip of tape down the outside of the drinking glass.

2. Starting at the bottom of the tape strip, measure the height of the strip in centimeters. Write this measurement on the top of the strip of tape.

3. Scrape the glass across the snow to fill it, then level the top of the snow in the glass by scraping the edge of the ruler across the mouth of the glass. Take care not to pack the snow in the cup. Fresh snow works best.

4. Allow the filled glass to sit at room temperature until the snow melts.

5. Mark the height of the water in the glass on the strip of tape. Measure this height in centimeters and write it on the tape. Compare the height of the snow to the height of the water it forms when melted.

Results

The glass of melted snow produces less than one glass of water. The height of the snow in the author's glass was 15 cm and the height of the water was 1.5 cm.

Why?

As the snow crystals fall through the atmosphere, they cluster together and form snowflakes. A lot of air also mixes with the snowflakes as the flakes fall to the ground. The more air is mixed with the snow, the greater the volume of the snow. When the snow melts,

the air in the mixture is released. The volume of snow is greater than the volume of liquid water it forms when melted. Shaved or crushed ice is also a mixture of small ice crystals and air. It, like the snow, has a greater volume than the water it forms when melted. Snow containing lots of trapped air will be very fluffy and insulating, but when melted it will produce less water than the same amount of denser snow.

MORE FUN WITH SNOW!

See for yourself that trapped air in snow is a good insulator by comparing the insulating properties of paper (material without air) and styrofoam (material with air). Put an ice cube inside a paper cup, then slip a second paper cup of equal size inside the first one so that it rests on top of the ice cube. Repeat, but use two styrofoam cups the same size as the paper cups and an ice cube the same size as the one in the paper cups. Lift the top cups and observe the ice cubes once every 5 minutes. Continue until one of the ice cubes completely melts.

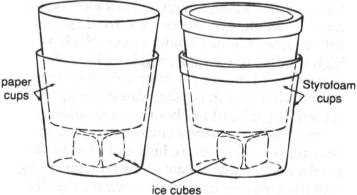

BOOK LIST

Archer, Cheryl. *Snow Watch*. Buffalo, N.Y.: Kids Can Press, 1997. Fun indoor and outdoor activities about snow, as well as information about snowflake formation, how to catch a snowflake and keep it, and much, much more.

VanCleave, Janice. *Weather*. New York: Wiley, 1995. Experiments about snow and other weather topics. Each chapter contains ideas that can be turned into award-winning science fair projects.

Winds

Highland (alpine) tundra begins at the timber-line on mountains. The patchy forest of short, bent trees bordering the tundra is called **krummholz** (German for "crooked wood"). These trees, usually low, bent, wind-shaped spruce and fir trees, are not a special species, instead the same trees if grown at a lower elevation where there is less wind would be taller and straighter.

Wind is the movement of air from one place to another in a direction relatively parallel to Earth's surface. Winds are produced by differences in atmospheric pressure, which are primarily due to differences in temperature. Persistent winds are a feature of both the low-land and highland tundras. Winds in highland tundras are due primarily to differences in air temperature between high and low elevations. Since tundra temperatures vary, wind speeds will vary, but highland tundra generally have high winds. For example, winds of 45 to 65 miles (74 to 105 km) per hour are common on Mount McKinley in Alaska, with gusts up to 100 miles (160 km) per hour even in summer.

In a cold, very windy environment, organisms must produce more heat and have better insulation and other adaptations for conserving heat than organisms living in a warm, slightly windy environment. This is because the body heat at the surface of an animal's skin is carried away by wind. The faster the wind, the faster it carries heat away from surfaces it passes over.

Winds also dry surfaces they pass over by speeding up evaporation of water from the surfaces. Some plants in the tundra have a waxy coating, much like desert plants, which prevents water loss as well as helps to keep the plant warm.

Winds also pick up particles of dirt, ice, and snow that grind away surfaces they hit, much the way sandpaper grinds away surfaces it is rubbed against. Animals can hide behind rocks and live in underground dwellings to protect themselves from the abrasive winds. Rocks also protect plants from the wind, and at times snow covers and protects above-ground plant parts.

FUN TIME!

Purpose

To demonstrate the cooling effect of wind.

Materials

you

Procedure

1. Hold the back of your hand close to, but not touching, your mouth.

2. Open your mouth and blow as hard as possible. Observe how warm or cold your breath makes your hand feel.

3. Repeat steps 1 and 2, pursing your lips.

Results

Your hand feels warmer when you blow on it with an open mouth and cooler when you blow on it through pursed lips.

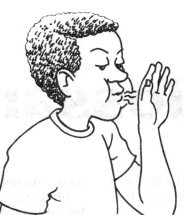

Why?

The temperature of your breath is the same whether your mouth is open or your lips are pursed. The difference in the perceived temperature is that with your mouth open your warm breath comes out slowly, gently pushing away the air layer above your hand and taking its place. Since your breath is warmer than the air layer, your skin feels warmer. But when you purse your lips, the air is forced through a smaller opening and comes out of your mouth more rapidly. The faster-moving air blows away the air layer above your hand, allowing cooler air from the room to move in. This makes your skin feel cooler.

MORE FUN WITH WIND!

Wind chill is a measure of the cooling effect of wind. Wind doesn't make the air temperature lower, instead it increases the rate at which a body loses heat. So the air on a windy day feels cooler than the temperature indicated by a thermometer. The wind-chill equivalent temperature is determined by the relationship between the speed of the wind and the temperature of the air. The wind-chill equivalent temperature is the temperature calm air would have to be to produce the same equivalent cooling of exposed skin. For example, to determine the wind-chill equivalent temperature for a wind speed of 40 miles per hour and an air temperature of 5°F, find 40 miles per hour on the vertical axis of the Wind Chill Table. Follow the row of numbers over until they are in line with the column beneath the air temperature of 5°F. Where the wind speed row and temperature column meet is the number, –45, which is the equivalent temperature of –45°F. With a wind speed of 40 miles per hour and an air temperature of 5°F, you would feel as though the air temperature were –45°F.

In cold weather, exposure to this excessive cooling due to wind chill can lead to **hypothermia**, a lowering of the body temperature of animals that can cause death. Important chemical processes in both plants and animals occur more slowly at cold temperatures and will not occur at all if the temperature is too low. Plants and animals in the tundra have special adaptations in order to survive in this cold windy environment.

Wind Chill Table

WIND SPEED (MILES PER HOUR)	AIR TEMPERATURE (°F)																
	35	30	25	20	15	10	5	0	–5	–10	–15	–20	–25	–30	–35	–40	–45
0-4	35	30	25	20	15	10	5	0	–5	–10	–15	–20	–25	–30	–35	–40	–45
5	32	27	22	16	11	6	0	–5	–10	–15	–21	–26	–31	–36	–42	–47	–52
10	22	16	10	3	–3	–9	–15	–22	–27	–34	–40	–46	–52	–58	–64	–71	–77
15	16	9	2	–5	–11	–18	–25	–31	–38	–45	–51	–58	–65	–72	–78	–85	–92
20	12	4	–3	–10	–17	–24	–31	–39	–46	–53	–60	–67	–74	–81	–88	–95	–103
25	8	1	–7	–15	–22	–29	–36	–44	–51	–59	–66	–74	–81	–88	–96	–103	–110
30	6	–2	–10	–18	–25	–33	–41	–49	–56	–64	–71	–79	–86	–93	–101	–109	–116
35	4	–4	–12	–20	–27	–35	–43	–52	–58	–67	–74	–82	–89	–97	–105	–113	–120
40	3	–5	–13	–21	–29	–37	–45	–53	–60	–69	–76	–84	–92	–100	–107	–115	–123
45	2	–6	–14	–22	–30	–38	–46	–54	–62	–70	–78	–85	–93	–102	–109	–117	–125

BOOK LIST

Mandell, Muriel. *Simple Weather Experiments with Everyday Materials.* New York: Sterling Publishing Co., Inc. 1991. Exciting experiments that show amazing facts behind wind-chill and other weather-related topics.

VanCleave, Janice. *Weather.* New York: Wiley, 1995. Experiments about wind and other weather-related topics. Each chapter contains ideas that can be turned into award-winning science fair projects.

Glossary

abscission layer   The layer of cells at the base of a leaf's petiole that cuts the leaf from the stem as the plant prepares for winter.

absorb   To take in.

accelerate   To increase in speed.

accretion   The method by which a water drop grows as various water drops bump into one another and merge.

active layer   The surface layer of permafrost that thaws and refreezes each year.

adaptation   A structure or behavior that helps an organism survive in its environment.

air current   The motion of air in a vertical, or nearly vertical, direction.

alpine tundra   Tundra at high altitudes; also called highland tundra.

alternate   A leaf arrangement pattern in which one leaf grows from each node in a stair-step pattern from one side to the other along the stem.

angiosperms   Flowering plants.

annual evaporation rate   A measure of how much moisture evaporates from the surface each year.

annuals   Plants that live for only one year or growing season.

Antarctic   The region south of the Antarctic Circle.

Antarctic Circle   The latitude at 66½°S.

anthocyanin   A red plant pigment.

arid   Dry.

Arctic   The region north of the Arctic Circle.

Arctic Circle   The latitude at 66½°N.

Arctic tundra   Lowland tundra in the Arctic.

atmosphere   In reference to Earth, it is the blanket of gas surrounding the planet.

atmospheric pressure   The force that air in the atmosphere exerts on a particular area.

autumn   A climatic season with medium-length cool days.

autumnal equinox   The first day of autumn, on or about September 23 in the Northern Hemisphere.

axis   An imaginary line through the center of an object about which the object turns.

basal metabolism   The amount of energy used by the body while resting or fasting to carry out basic functions, such as breathing, making your heart pump, and growth.

biomes   Geographical regions identified by their dominant plants, their animals, and a particular climate.

blade   The flat part of a leaf.

blubber   A thick layer of fat beneath the skin of animals.

body mass index (BMI)   The ratio of body weight (in kilograms) to height (in meters).

boreal forest   See **coniferous forest**.

branch   A stem that grows out of a trunk.

broadleaf   A type of leaf that has a broad, flat shape.

buttresses   Thick roots that spread horizontally just above the ground.

camouflage   Colors or patterns that conceal an object by making it blend in with its background.

campos   The name of temperate grasslands of Uruguay and Brazil.

canopy layer   A forest's second layer, or roof, consisting of a network of branches and leaves, that form a covering that blocks some of the sunlight from reaching lower plants.

carbon dioxide   Gas in the air used by plants to produce food.

carnivore   A flesh-eating animal; a secondary consumer that belongs to the third trophic level.

carotene   A plant pigment that produces yellow-orange colors.

chlorophyll   A green pigment located in the chloroplasts of plants that is used to produce food.

climate   The average weather in a region over a long period of time.

climatic savannas   Savannas that result from climatic conditions.

climatic seasons   Divisions of the year based on average temperature and the amount of time that the Sun is in the sky each day.

cloud A visible mass of water droplets that float in the air, usually high above the earth.

cloud droplets Tiny drops of water with diameters between 0.00004 to 0.002 inches (0.0001 and 0.005 cm) that form clouds.

cold desert A desert whose daytime temperature is often below freezing for part of the year.

compacted Squeezed together.

compound leaf A leaf that has more than one blade on a petiole.

compressed Pushed together.

condense A change from a gas to a liquid.

cone Seed-bearing structure; where the seeds of gymnosperms are produced.

conifer Plants with seed-bearing structures called cones; gymnosperms, such as pines.

coniferous forest A forest of coniferous trees found in the Northern Hemisphere north of the temperate forests; also called a boreal forest or taiga.

consumers Organisms that cannot produce their own food, so they have to feed on other organisms.

crops Plants grown for food.

crown Leaves and branches that make up a tree's leafy head.

crystal A solid material whose particles are arranged in a repeating pattern.

deciduous Plants that lose all their leaves during part of the year.

deciduous forest A biome characterized by deciduous trees found in a region with a temperate climate.

decomposer An organism that gets its nutrients by breaking down the chemicals in waste and dead organisms.

decomposition The breakdown of substances into simpler parts, such as the decay of plants and animals.

den A shelter for animals in nature.

dense Having parts closely packed together.

density A measure of the mass of a given volume of material.

desert An arid biome that receives fewer than 10 inches (25 cm) of rainfall a year.

dew Water from water vapor in the air that condenses on cool surfaces.

discontinuous Interrupted.

dissolve To break up and thoroughly mix with another substance.

diurnal animals Animals that feed during the day.

domesticated Tamed to live with or be used by humans.

dormant Alive but inactive.

drought A time when there is a lack of rain.

drought-deciduous Desert plants that sprout leaves only during the rainy period, then drop them when it gets dry.

dry season A seasonal change when there is a lack of rain.

dune fields Areas with many sand dunes.

ecosystem A certain place and the living and non-living things found there.

egg A female reproductive cell.

elevation The height above sea level.

emergent layer A rain forest's upper layer, made up of the tallest trees.

endangered species An organism that is in danger of extinction.

environment All the living and nonliving surroundings of an organism.

ephemeral An annual desert plant that lives for a short time.

equator An imaginary line that divides Earth into two parts, called the Northern and Southern Hemispheres; latitude 0°.

erosion The process by which materials of Earth's surface are broken down and carried away by natural agents, such as wind and water.

estivation The dormant condition of some desert animals that sleep through the hot summer when there is not enough food.

evaporation The change from a liquid to a gas.

evergreens Plants that do not lose all their leaves during the year; plants that retain individual leaves for one or more consecutive years.

external ear The part of the ear on the outside of your head.

extinction The dying off of all individuals of a species.

fasting Not eating.

fauna The animals of a certain region.

fertile soil Soil that contains an abundance of humus.

fibrous roots Roots that have no main section but spread out into the soil in all directions.

fledgling A young bird with feathers necessary for flight.

flora The plant life of a certain region.

fluid A gas or a liquid.

fog A cloud that is close to the ground.

fog desert A high-pressure desert covered with fog.

food chain   A   model that shows how a group of organisms are linked together in the order in which they feed on one another; the order of the transfer of nutritional energy in an environment.

food pyramid   A pyramid-shaped model that compares the organisms in each level of a food chain.

food web   All the possible food patterns in an ecosystem.

forest   A terrestrial biome in which trees are the main plant.

forest floor   The bottom layer of a forest.

germinate   Begin to grow.

glide   To fly without engine power.

grass   A nonwoody, usually green plant with long, thin, erect leaves.

grassland   A biome in which the dominant plant is grass.

graze   To feed on growing grass.

gymnosperm   A nonflowering seed plant that reproduces by seeds on the scales of a cone.

halophytic   Plants that are tolerant of salts in the soil.

hardwood   Wood from broadleafed trees.

heat   Energy that is transferred from a warm material to a cool material.

heliotropic   In plants, having the ability to turn to face the Sun to gather more light and warmth.

herbaceous   Nonwoody, with relatively soft stems.

herbivore   An animal that eats only plants; the first consumer or primary consumer in a food chain.

hibernation   Dormant condition of some animals that sleep through the winter.

highland tundra   See **alpine tundra**.

high-pressure desert   A desert formed as a result of high atmospheric pressure.

hot deserts   Deserts whose daytime temperatures are generally very hot.

humidity   The measure of the amount of water vapor in the air.

humus   Material in soil formed by decayed plants and animals.

hygroscopic   Able to absorb water from the air.

hypothermia   A lowering of the body temperature of animals that can cause death.

inactive layer   The layer of permafrost that does not thaw.

infertile soil   Soil lacking nutrients.

inland desert   A desert that forms because the air that sweep over the area is dry and there isn't another source of moisture.

insulator   A material that offers a great resistance to the flow of heat into or out of it.

krummholz   The patchy forest of short, bent trees bordering the tundra.

latitude   An imaginary line that gives the location of a place north (N) or south (S) of the Earth's equator and is expressed in degrees.

leaching   In reference to soil, it is the process of washing away nutrients by runoff.

leaflet   One of the blades on a compound leaf.

leaves   The main food-producing part of a plant.

lowland tundra   See **Arctic tundra.**

migration   A periodic movement of animals in response to changes in climate or food availability.

monsoon rain forests   Areas that experience pronounced wet and dry seasons.

nectar   A sugary liquid in flowers.

nocturnal animals   Animals that are active at night.

node   A point in a plant stem where a leaf is generally attached.

Northern Hemisphere   The region of Earth that is north of the equator.

northern tropics   The region of Earth that lies between the equator and the Tropic of Cancer.

North Pole   The north end of Earth's axis.

north temperate zone   The region of Earth between the Tropic of Cancer and the Arctic Circle.

nutrients   Nourishing materials needed for life.

obesity   The condition of being overweight.

omnivore   An animal that eats plants or other animals; a secondary consumer that belongs to the second and third trophic levels.

opposite   Leaf arrangement pattern, in which two leaves grow from the same node, one on either side of the stem.

orbit   The curved path of one body about another, such as that of Earth about the Sun.

organisms   Living things.

pampas   The name of temperate grasslands in Argentina.

partially deciduous   Plants that lose part but not all of their leaves each year.

perennial   A plant that lives many years.

permafrost   Ground that is frozen.

permafrost table   The surface of an inactive layer of permafrost.

petiole   The part of a plant that holds a leaf to a branch.

photosynthesis   The process by which plants use chlorophyll and light energy, generally sunlight, to manufacture food from water and carbon dioxide.

pigment   A chemical that gives a substance color because it absorbs, reflects, and transmits a specific color of light.

plantigrade feet   Feet whose heel and sole touch the ground when an animal or human walks.

pollen   Tiny capsules that contain the male reproductive cells.

pollen cone   A cone that contains pollen.

prairie   The name of temperate grasslands in North America.

precipitation   Water that falls from the atmosphere in the form of rain, hail, snow, or sleet.

predator   An animal that kills and eats other animals.

primary consumer   An animal that feeds on plants; herbivore; belongs to the second trophic level.

primary producers   Plants that provide food for primary consumers; belongs to the first trophic level.

producers   Organisms in a food chain that can use nonliving materials to produce food; plants.

psychrometer   An instrument used to measure relative humidity.

pure grasslands   Grasslands made up only of grasses.

pyramid of number   A food pyramid in which the numbers of organisms decrease as you move up the food chain from the producer to the top consumer.

rain forests   Forests that have a constant warm temperature and abundant rainfall throughout the year.

rain-shadow desert   A desert that forms on the side of a mountain away from an ocean.

rangeland   The name of temperate grasslands of Australia and New Zealand.

rehydrate   To restore moisture.

relative humidity   The amount of water vapor in the air compared to the total amount of vapor that the air could hold at that temperature, expressed as a percentage.

revolve   To move in a curved path around another object; to move around a central point, as the planets move around the Sun.

rhizomes   Horizontal stems that grow below ground.

roots   The part of a plant that anchors it in the ground; usually below the ground but some are above ground. See **stilted roots** and **buttresses.**

rotation   The turning of an object about its axis.

runners   See **stolons.**

runoff   Rainwater that is unable to soak into the ground and moves over its surface.

sand dunes   Hills of loose sand.

sandstone   A type of rock made from a buildup of layers of sand.

saturated   Soaked; not able to hold any more fluid, such as air that is filled with water vapor.

savannas   Tropical grasslands with scattered trees.

seasons   Divisions of the year defined by the position of Earth as it moves about the Sun, weather, and rainfall; divisions of the year based on average temperature and the amount of time that the sun is in the sky each day.

secondary consumer   An animal that eats another animal; belongs to the third trophic level.

seed   The part of a plant from which a new plant grows.

seed cone   A cone that contains seeds.

sexual reproduction   The union of a sperm and an egg.

sheath   For grass, it is the part that supports the blade by wrapping partially around the base of the blade.

shrub   A short, woody plant with several main stems instead of one main supportive stem called a trunk; a bush.

simple leaf   A leaf with one blade per petiole.

snow   Transparent ice crystals formed around dust or other small particles in the atmosphere when water vapor condenses at temperatures below the freezing point.

softwood   Wood from coniferous trees.

soil   The top layer of Earth's surface that supports plant life. It is composed of particles from rock mixed with humus.

solar energy   Energy from the Sun, including light and heat.

soluble   The ability of a substance to dissolve.

Southern Hemisphere   The region of Earth south of the equator.

South Pole   The south end of Earth's axis.

south temperate zone   The region of Earth between the Tropic of Capricorn and the Antarctic Circle.

southern tropics   The region of Earth that lies between the equator and the Tropic of Capricorn.

species   Specific types of organisms.

sperm   Male reproductive cells.

spring   A climatic season with medium-length warm days.

stem The part of a plant that supports the leaves and flowers and transports nutrients.

steppes The name of temperate grasslands of Central Eurasia.

stilted roots Roots that start at about 3 to 4 feet (0.9 to 1.2 m) high on the trunk and grow down into the ground.

stolons Horizontal stems that grow above ground; commonly called runners.

stomata Tiny surface openings that are especially abundant on the undersides of leaves.

streamlined Shaped to offer the least resistance to motion through fluids.

subcanopy A forest's layer beneath the canopy.

sublimation The process of a vapor changing directly to a solid without becoming a liquid.

succulent A plant in any biome with thick and fleshy stems or leaves designed to retain water and reduce evaporation.

summer A climatic season with long hot days.

summer solstice The first day of summer; on or about June 21 in the Northern Hemisphere and December 21 in the Southern Hemisphere.

taiga See **coniferous forest.**

temperate climate A climate without extremes in temperature or precipitation and with cool winters and warm summers of about equal length.

temperate deciduous forest A deciduous forest in a temperate zone.

temperate grassland Grassland in the temperate zones that have climate seasons.

temperate zones Regions north and south of the tropics. See **north temperate zone** and **south temperate zone.**

terrestrial Land.

terrestrial biomes Biomes found on land.

tertiary consumer A carnivore that eats other carnivores; belongs to the fourth trophic level.

timberline The line in northern latitudes above which no trees grow.

top carnivore The carnivore at the top level of a trophic level.

topography A description of the size, the shape, and the elevation of a region of land.

transparent Material that light easily passes through.

transpiration The evaporation of water from a plant's stomata.

trees Woody plants with a main supportive stem called a trunk.

trophic level Food levels showing the energy flow through a food chain from a producer to the top consumer.

tropical forest A forest located in the tropics.

tropical grassland Grasslands in the tropic regions where seasonal changes are based more on rainfall than temperature and thus have wet and dry seasons.

tropical rain forest A rain forest in the tropics that receives more than 80 inches (200 cm) of rain each year.

Tropic of Cancer The latitude at 23½°N.

Tropic of Capricorn The latitude at 23½°S.

tropics Two regions forming a band around the center of Earth; the region between the Tropic of Cancer and the Tropic of Capricorn.

trunk The main supportive stem of a plant.

tundra A treeless biome that occurs in areas where the winters are long and cold and the summers are usually cool and short; see **alpine tundra** and **Arctic tundra.**

ultimate consumer The top consumer in a trophic level.

vapor The gaseous state of a substance, such as water, that is normally in a liquid state.

veldts The name of temperate grasslands of South Africa.

vernal equinox The first day of spring, on or about March 21 in the Northern Hemisphere.

weather The condition of the atmosphere in a specific region at a particular time.

weathering The breaking apart of materials, such as rock. The part of erosion that involves only the breakdown of materials into smaller parts.

wet season A seasonal change when there is an abundance of rain.

whorled Arrangement of three or more leaves growing from one node.

wind The movement of air from one place to another in a direction relatively parallel to Earth's surface.

wind chill A measure of the cooling effect of wind.

winter A climatic season with short cold days.

winter solstice The first day of winter, on or about December 21 in the Northern Hemisphere and June 22 in the Southern Hemisphere.

wood The part of a plant made of xylem tubes; the hard, tough substance that forms the trunks of trees.

woody plant A plant with a large amount of wood.

xanthophyll A plant pigment that produces yellow colors.

xerophytes Plants that are adapted to grow in dry conditions.

xylem tubes Tubes that transport water and other nutrients from the root throughout a plant and provide support; wood.

Index